PORTRAIT OF SOUTH WALES

Also by Michael Senior

PORTRAIT OF NORTH WALES

Portrait of
SOUTH WALES

MICHAEL SENIOR

ROBERT HALE · LONDON

© Michael Senior 1974
First published in Great Britain 1974

ISBN 0 7091 4721 X

Robert Hale & Company
63 Old Brompton Road
London SW 7

Composed by Specialised Offset Services Ltd., Liverpool
and printed in Great Britain by
Lowe & Brydone Ltd., Thetford

CONTENTS

ILLUSTRATIONS

MAPS

CREDITS

The illustrations numbered 1, 6, 7 and 13 were taken by the author. The remaining photographs were supplied by the following: Peter Baker Photography (2, 4, 5, 12, 18, 19, 23, 24, 26, 27); Ron Chapman (8, 9, 10, 11, 16, 17, 20, 21, 22, 25); Ednyfed Hudson Davies (3); Sheelah Latham (14, 15).

ACKNOWLEDGEMENTS

The author wishes to thank J.M. Dent and Sons Ltd for permission to quote extracts from *The Itinerary Through Wales* and *Description of Wales* by Giraldus Cambrensis and from *Dylan Thomas in America* by J.M. Brinnin; Professor Gwyn Jones and Mrs Mair Jones for permission to quote extracts from their translation of the *Mabinogion*; David Higham Associates and J.M. Dent and Sons Ltd for permission to quote from *Collected Poems, Quite Early One Morning* and *A Prospect of the Sea* by Dylan Thomas; Penguin Books Ltd for permission to quote from *The History of the Kings of Britain* by Geoffrey of Monmouth translated by Lewis Thorpe; and Jonathan Cape Ltd and Mrs H.M. Davies for permission to quote from *The Autobiography of a Super-Tramp* by W.H. Davies.

INTRODUCTION

DEHEUBARTH AND OTHER KINGDOMS

As a species, we love dividing things up; chopping the natural continuum into classes and orders and, of course, giving them names. Caesar did it to Gaul; and in fact Wales shows no resistance to being split into three parts. Perhaps it is fissile by nature.

> Wales was in ancient times divided into three parts nearly equal, consideration having been paid, in this division, more to the value than to the just quantity or proportion of territory. They were Venedotia, now called North Wales; Demetia, or South Wales, which is in British called Deheubarth, that is, the southern part; and Powys, the middle or eastern district.

In ancient times. Giraldus, writing in about 1188, was no doubt referring to the Roman classification, which in turn was based on the tribal territories, their names simply being latinized. The question of whether Wales would really be viewed as one, two or three units has never fully been discussed. The Tourist Board, for instance, in modern times treat it as three. A number of those who fear for its national identity would like to see it viewed as one. If it had not already been done in another context we might take the analogy-bearing shamrock for our symbol. It is three in one and one in three.

Portrait of North Wales, the companion volume to this one, stopped, with a certain air of arbitrariness, at Barmouth. One has to stop somewhere, and with as much logic and as little apology this book begins again at Cardigan. Why the hiatus? What is it about Machynlleth and Aberystwyth that makes it necessary to leave them in limbo? The fact is that of

the three parts of Wales which have, one way and another,,
come to be recognized as independent sections, the middle
one by comparison with the north and south contains, for all
its beauty and deep-engrained character, rather less of the
variety and close-packed background detail which are essential, as a minimum requirement, to support a book.

South Wales is not now, and never has been, a single simple
place. In the course of its short distances one goes from the
extreme of rural wilderness to the equally polarized depths of
industrial suburbanism. The course is a zig-zag one through
the spectrum of human land-use, and the pattern of this book
reflects it. In South Wales you are never for long firmly in
one world or the other. The grass banks of the mountain
come down to the very gates of the back-yards of those miles
and miles of terraced houses. The billowing chimneys of
power stations or steel works, the clustered domes of
refineries, squat beyond the hill of a placid coastal landscape.
Wild countryside almost invades Cardiff's outskirts. The Vale
of Glamorgan quietly ignores the Rhondda and its influences
running down towards it. On an empty stretch of moor at the
neck of Gower, with no town of any sort to be seen, a notice
proclaims the boundary of Swansea City. And the view across
the bay from Mumbles illustrates a point which we might, in
a reaction to the material progress of the last century and of
this one, have overlooked. That is: that great cities and their
associated industries are part of our landscape, and there is
no aesthetic or moral principle which demands, as axiomatic,
that we must view them as being ugly.

South Wales is, in its way, as varied and full of contrasts as
is the North; more so perhaps because the impressions are
stronger and more emotively loaded. It was split, from the
beginning of its habitation, into a number of different
kingdoms, and to a large extent these divisions represent both
the natural distinctions and the present day differences
between one area of it and another.

From the Tywi westwards and from the Teifi southwards
(that is, with Carmarthen and Cardigan forming its border)
extended the tribal area of Demetia, which became, by the
seventh century, the kingdom of Dyfed. The term 'West
Wales' was originally used to refer to what is now Cornwall,

at the time when the Brythonic areas of Britain, together with Brittany, retained some cohesion. Now it is convenient, and has become customary, to transfer its use to this area of Dyfed, which is indeed the most westerly part of Wales.

To this nucleus was added the southern part of the kingdom of Seisyllwg, which stretched (as both modern Dyfed and Powys do today) sufficiently far northward to obliterate the distinction between South and Mid Wales. By the time of Gruffydd ap Llewelyn (1039–63), a prince who ruled most of Wales, the large and portentous kingdom of Deheubarth was recognizably formed.

This left three smaller kingdoms. Brycheiniog (the area now occupied by the Brecon Beacons National Park, together with Mynydd Epynt), Morgannwg, and Gwent. These last two, respectively, filled most of the present counties of Glamorgan, and the new county of Gwent. South Wales, then, has not greatly changed its structural make-up, the new divisions conforming to the areas laid down in post-Roman, pre-Norman times and maintained throughout the Middle Ages.

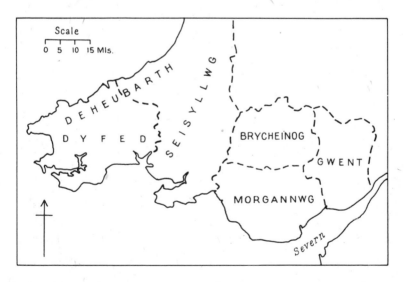

The Old Kingdoms

The name of Dyfed has now extended its use to include much of the former kingdom of Deheubarth, reversing the historical process by which the latter had absorbed the former. Part of Deheubarth however has now become West Glamorgan. Brycheiniog is almost entirely absorbed in the large central county of Powys; and Morgannwg as it was is split into two further divisions of Glamorgan, Mid and South. To a large extent the older county names, imposed on Wales by Edward I, continue, and are likely to continue for some time, to be used. So that it is meaningful to talk still of distinctions between Pembrokeshire, Carmarthenshire and Cardiganshire, even now that, as legal entities, these have gone out of existence.

The population of South Wales became mixed at an early date. Indeed it is likely that a strong Irish influence had spread into Dyfed even before the formation of the king-doms. Certainly Giraldus assumed that it was not a new idea that the north contained a less mixed population than the south. It is, then, probable that this long tradition of immigration has had some effect on the character of the people.

The New Counties

INTRODUCTION   15

It seems, for one thing, that a people's time-perspective has some correlation to their state in space, of movement or fixity, and that their view of the past (when they have one) is long-focus or close-range according to the length of time that they, as a community, have been wherever they are. In parts of North Wales it is still sometimes considered worth a mention that a person comes from another valley. In the county of Glamorgan between 1861 and the end of that century some 300,000 people came from another valley. It is, consequently, to different seismic disturbances that the rumblings of that Welsh dissatisfaction which they have in common is related. In South Wales they sometimes think, or feel, not in terms of those cataclysmic events of the thirteenth century, but of things which are well within the first-hand memory of their grandfathers. Not the humiliation of poor Llewelyn's head on its pike, and the raising of the fortresses of the Plantagenet conqueror; but the lock-outs and the dole queues, and the election of Keir Hardie in the Merthyr Tydfil constituency at the dawn of this desolate or splendid century.

There were two peaks of immigration, corresponding to economic conditions both in South Wales and elsewhere. Between 1881 and 1891, over a hundred thousand people moved into Glamorgan. Between 1901 and 1911 the number moving in reached 128,500. Many, at the same time, were moving out; such is the baffling nature of economic demography. A sudden decline in the iron industry, for instance, led to large-scale emigration during the 1870s, when 15,000 people left Glamorgan, a large amount of them forming the Welsh emigration to Pennsylvania. The net gain by migration can be arrived at by finding the excess of actual increase over natural increase, and during the two peaks mentioned it was, in the first, 77,000, and in the second more than 92,000. During the whole period (1861–1911) the population of part of South Wales had actually grown by some 259,000 people over and above the natural increase.

The population of South Wales now is about 1.8 million, and that of the whole of Wales some two and three-quarter million. Sixty-five percent of the population of the whole of Wales lives in perhaps less than one quarter of its area.

Industrialization was not new to South Wales in the mid-nineteenth century. There were brass foundries in Monmouthshire at an early date, and copper-smelting took place at Neath in the reign of Edward I. During the seventeenth century lead was mined in Cardiganshire, and iron began to be worked, at that time, at Pontypool. By the end of the eighteenth century the four great ironworks at Merthyr were established, and ironworking spread into the Monmouthshire valleys. To begin with the foundries had been fuelled by wood, but the forests which once covered the upper ends of the valleys soon began to run out. And it hardly needs to be said that it was the presence of the coalfield which led to the expansion of the iron industry during the nineteenth century.

The coalfield is a fifty-six-mile long, oval-shaped belt, stretching from Carmarthen Bay to Pontypool. It is, in general, up to sixteen miles wide. It is not a single uniform stretch of strata, but consists of several different types of coal, the qualities and characteristics of which have had considerable historical effect on the social and economic make-up of the area. Bituminous and steam coals stretch in two separate bands down the eastern boundary and round the southern side of the belt. In the middle are smokeless and dry-steam coals. To the west, and occupying the northern area around Ammanford, are the anthracites and semi-anthracites. The strata are, throughout, nearest to the surface along the rim of the oval-shaped field, and dip deeper towards the centre.

In spite of the images which one has, it is not the case that coal was the principle material of trade which led to the expansion of South Wales. It became so only relatively late in the country's swift development, and remained so only for a comparatively short period. The rise of the area's prosperity and population relied mainly on iron. There is a mutual relationship between iron and war, and the war in America undoubtedly gave the industry an impetus at the end of the eighteenth century without which it might not have launched so strongly into the nineteenth. The Seven Years War (1756–1763) had perhaps originally set it on its feet. And the wars with France led to a further demand for munitions during the 1790s.

There is, moreover, a comparable relationship between the iron industry and the railways, and in fact each of them would have had great difficulty in realizing their fast expansion without the other one. It was a side-effect of this that the rail and tram roads which carried the iron from the mines and foundries (on iron rails) during the middle of the nineteenth century also (like the foundries themselves) gave rise to an increasing demand for steam coal. The fact is that Watt's improved steam engine of the 1780s led to both a new form of transport for both iron and coal and a new demand for both of these commodities. Railways carried them down to the ports, from which coal-burning steamships carried them abroad. As long as people were still building railways the two industries flourished; America and Russia were constructing their early railroads with Welsh iron during the mid-1840s.

In the meantime a small amount of trade in coal itself, for purposes other than fuelling transport, had begun to grow. It took some time, however, for the kingdoms of the iron kings to be replaced by the mine-owners' empires which dominated South Wales in the later period of its expansion. Until the rise of the railways the only towns which received Welsh coal for domestic purposes were those easily reached by river or canal, and to begin with the market extended no further than Bristol. The quality of Welsh coal, however, came to be appreciated in London, which had been bringing its coals from Newcastle. Welsh 'smokeless' coal, from the Merthyr area, was recognizably less smoky. In 1829 more than 2,000 tons were exported from Cardiff, mainly to London. In the 1830s the French market began to open up, and the rise of the docks at Cardiff and Barry were an end result of this new trade. By 1881 Cardiff was the biggest coal-exporting port in the world.

Two main factors checked the steady advance of South Wales. The railways were largely finished by 1860, and those that were still being built turned, during the 1870s, to the new material, steel.

The invention of steel in the 1850s had an inevitable effect on the state of South Wales; but it proved, as it turned out, the tenacity with which an industry once established will remain in place. The ironworks mostly converted to the steel-making process during the 1880s, and continued to flourish. It is remarkable that they should have done so, since their existence had originally been due to the presence near at hand of suitable ores for making iron, and these were no longer of any use. The local iron-ore contained too much phosphorus, which the process was unable to eliminate. Foreign ores, which in any case were richer, had to be imported; and the town of Bilbao in northern Spain owes much of its rise to prominence to this chance.

The ironworks and their towns, however, had grown around the northern rim of the coalfield, because that was where the iron mines were. The need to carry up imported ores led to a sharp rise in costs at Merthyr, and many of the large works were faced with the alternatives of closing or moving. Several of the major concerns then turned entirely to coal production. Towards the end of the century the demand for coal for use in steam-powered factories and for fuelling transport increased, and coal became a major industry. The Upper Rhondda and the Aberdare valley were developed almost entirely from this period onwards.

In 1891 the Dowlais works, which had changed to making steel shortly after the discovery of the process in 1856, moved down to East Moors, near Cardiff. In 1890 Barry Docks had opened, to deal with the expansion of the coal trade. The pattern of development had changed, and the north and east of the coalfield then declined. The centres of economic balance moved to the anthracite coalfield and the ports.

Iron and coal were not the only minerals exploited during this short and dramatic period. Copper-smelting had been fundamental to Swansea's and Llanelli's economy from an early date, being, as local ores declined, partly replaced by tin-plate manufacture. Its peak was at about 1860, when Swansea dominated world trade in copper. The area continued, using imported ores, to keep its place in the market during the 1880s; another striking instance of the ability of an industry to survive even after its original basis has gone. But by 1890 the producers of the raw material which Swansea was importing had started to build smelters of their own. America became self-supplying in copper and tin, and Australia and Chile started smelting their own ores in preference to sending them half-way round the world and buying back the product. The highly-specialized and localized nature of the industry made this decline of catastrophic importance to the population, and massive emigration resulted. When the coal industry, in its turn, declined, the situation in South Wales seemed to have gone further on the recoil than it had ever got on the initial swing.

The years of industrial unrest, which in any case was far from a new phenomenon in South Wales, have left the story with, in many people's minds, a bitter end. The fact is that the influx of the second half of the previous century had been too great. By 1928 there was a surplus of 55,000 workers in South Wales. Between 1921 and 1939 some 400,000 people left.

We are left now with a surprisingly pleasant place, to a large extent recovered from its unsettling eras of boom and depression. The manufacturing industries gained prominence during the 1960s, being larger now, in terms of jobs, than either mining or metal. Three-quarters of the jobs in Wales are in South Wales, and many of them are in the fields of vehicle-manufacture and engineering. Service industries also play a big part in the employment pattern, forming in fact the largest employment group, including a high proportion of women. The total labour force is not, in modern terms, a large one, and consequently diversification is inevitably limited. Economies of scale require large works, and it is estimated that ten giant works could absorb the workers of South Wales completely.

This is a preliminary outline of a complex and often confusing matter. There will be a chance to see some details of it, and of the people involved, in relation to the places they concern. At this stage one thing must be stressed, so much does the economic history of South Wales tend to outweigh its other qualities. Very much of the area is purely rural, maintaining an agricultural and peaceful life which bears little obvious relation to the sudden changes of the other parts, its neighbours.

In a progress of this kind it is inevitable that certain

themes and certain people keep recurring. They run through the strata like mineral seams, obtruding in places in the form of visible outcrops, in others struck below the surface by only a little probing. In North Wales, for instance, one such undercurrent was provided by George Borrow, indefatigably marching through the wilderness, noting down every detail of his journey, showing off his Welsh. He gave a point of reference, a historical perspective, in a country where visitors and their views have a good deal of relevance. In an equivalent position in South Wales stands Giraldus Cambrensis, who, some six centuries earlier, accompanied Archbishop Baldwin through Wales to gather recruits for the Third Crusade. What Giraldus provides is a constant reminder of the continuity of character and make-up which underlie the surface changes. He gives us a direct point of entry into the basal elements of the country; and much about it as it is today, it transpires, is far from new. In 1188, as now, South Wales was more accessible, more populated, more amenable to strangers, and more tamed, than was the north. And though it seems that Giraldus and Baldwin found it wise to scuttle fairly hastily through North Wales, in the south they lingered, hob-nobbing with the lords and hearing all the local scandal. Giraldus recorded it all, "the names of springs and torrents, the witty sayings, the toils and incidents of the journey, the memorable events of ancient and modern times, and the natural history and description of the country; lest my study should perish through idleness, or the praise of these things be lost by silence." For all its faults, probably no better source than this *Itinery* exists for the background of South Wales.

Giraldus came at the height of the Norman colonization of a major part of South Wales. Nationalistic consciousness was already fully developed, and both he and the people he spoke to were aware of the differences between those who had been moving into Wales and those whose ancestors had always been there. That too is something which hardly changes; though one may continue to wonder to what extent the people who had been moving in over these long periods became, eventually, absorbed into the Welshness of the native population, to come to share its national self-awareness. One thing is certain: however many nations invade it it stays Welsh. There is something intrinsic to the country which overcomes imported influences. The point was made effectively during the invasions of Henry II in the mid-twelfth century, by an old Welshman whose support for the king had not clouded his awareness of the impermeability of the situation. Asked by the king to comment, he said:

This nation, O king, may now, as in former times, be harassed, and in a great measure weakened and destroyed by your and other powers, and it will often prevail by its laudable exertions; but it can never be totally subdued through the wrath of man, unless the wrath of God shall concur. Nor do I think, that any other nation than this of Wales, or any other language, whatever may hereafter come to pass, shall, in the day of severe examination before the Supreme Judge, answer for this corner of the earth.

PART ONE

WEST WALES

I   THE TEIFI AND THE GWAUN

The A485 springs from an obscure source in the rolling
country south of Aberystwyth, and winds its way, joined by
branches from Cwm Ystwyth and Aberarth, down through
the humped land of northern Cardigan. The River Teifi runs
from close to Strata Florida, by a route complicated by
junctions and intersections, by-passing Tregaron and
Llanddewi Brefi. When they meet at Lampeter there is not
much sense of occasion. But it is perhaps their conjunction
here that marks the beginning of South Wales.

Lampeter is not obviously on the Teifi, which runs just
beyond its outskirts. The town sits to one side of the valley,
trim and tidy, clean and respectable, laid out with a sense of
purpose in a concise Victorian way. A worried reaction to
Methodism on the part of the Church of Wales caused the
founding there, in 1822, of a college for the education of
clergy. Lampeter's connection with education has remained
in place, and St David's College, a branch of the University of
Wales, gives the town a vitality which it might not otherwise
have had.

If, crossing the Teifi by Lampeter's bridge, one is now in
South Wales, it would be hard to tell from the visible data.
Nothing distinguishes the broad and rather shapeless Teifi
valley from other stretches of good Welsh farmland. The
small, thickly-hedged fields, the kestrels against the sunny,
woolly sky, the cattle in the fields mimicking those on the
roadsigns – square, black, immobile – and occasionally a
small and rural village nudging the road out of its alignment.
Somewhere in Wales. Sometime between the Middle Ages and
the Armageddon.

The Teifi is by no means grand or spectacular, but it has its

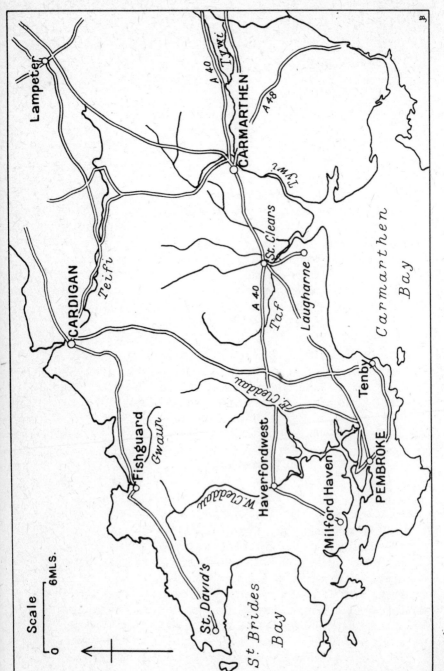

Scale
6 MLS.
0

St David's

St Brides Bay

Fishguard

Gwaun

St. Clears

Teifu

CARDIGAN

Lampeter

A 40

Tywi

CARMARTHEN

A 48

Tywi

A 40

Taf

Laugharne

Carmarthen Bay

Tenby

PEMBROKE

Milford Haven

Haverfordwest

W. Cleddau

E. Cleddau

West Wales

B

admirers. Giraldus called it "noble", chiefly on account of the quality of its salmon, which he said were fished productively near Cilgerran, as they still indeed are. Some things in this *Itinerary* serve as an accurate record of the present day. When he came down this valley there were certainly coracles on the Teifi, fishing the salmon with which it abounded. He described them, in fact, as being the craft used for this purpose: "made of twigs, not oblong nor pointed, but almost round, or rather triangular, covered both within and without with raw hides . . . The fishermen, according to the custom of the country, in going to and from the rivers, carry these boats on their shoulders."

From the 1180s to the 1970s is such a long time during which to continue to do something so fundamentally strange, that one is at first amazed to discover that they still carry down the same lath-constructed crafts from Cilgerran to the river. But the history of the coracle is even more impressive than this continuity indicates. When Giraldus saw them they were already an extremely ancient vehicle. Closely related to the Irish curragh, in which St Columba crossed to Iona in 563, and which fishermen still use in the choppy seas around the Irish islands, the coracle has its origins somewhere in the Iron Age, perhaps even forming a mode of transport by which the Celtic people originally arrived in Britain. Indeed when, about 2,500 B.C., the megalith-builders of the New Stone Age came northwards into Pembrokeshire, bringing with them some elementary agricultural skills, their boats were probably of the same lath-and-skin construction.

Some things, then, are so effective and so simple as to be ageless; one-and-a-half millennia of technological progress has no effect on them. There are coracles still on the Teifi and the Tywi, fishing the salmon with which both rivers abound. They are made, now, not with hides but with calico, stretched across a framework of willow-laths, woven across each other into the form of a sort of large basket. A sheet of cloth is fastened across it, and coated on the outside with a thick, waterproof layer of pitch. The vessel, completed, is extremely light and portable, which is perhaps one of the main reasons for its continuing usefulness. One man can carry one up and down the banks on his back, looking like a small version of those giant black beetles which Maurice O'Sullivan described on the beaches of the Blasket islands. When in use, they bob rather alarmingly on the eddying river; propelled by paddles, like a canoe but with a different motion, they are fast and easy to manoeuvre. The salmon fishers normally work in pairs, with a net, which is drawn across the salmon run at the right state of the water and the right time of the year.

The Teifi is bridged at Newcastle Emlyn – the castle referred to, a sixteenth-century fortress on a mound, over-looks the brown, stony river – and at Cenarth, where one may still sometimes see the coracles in use, at the point at which the river, after a short stretch of exuberance involving some small water-falls, pauses briefly for a period of big, eddying pools. And at Cilgerran, a little lower down, where the river runs through a deep, wooded gorge, a tourist-oriented speciality is made, in the summer, of the skills of coracle-handling.

Giraldus goes on to describe another oddity of the Teifi, but one which, unlike the salmon and coracles, no longer forms a feature of the otherwise changeless valley. It is, he says, the only river in England or Wales which has beavers. He leaves us in no doubt that it is indeed the animal we know as the beaver that he means – they have "broad, short tails, thick, like the palm of a hand, which they use as a rudder in swimming" – but engages in some fanciful descriptions of the methods by which they build their dams. Some of them lie on their backs to act as a sledge for the timber, which the others pull from the woods to the river.

The bridge at Cenarth hardly constitutes a village, beautiful and ancient though it is. Newcastle Emlyn, on the other hand, is compact and solid, clustered around its crossing place. Cilgerran, above the gorge, is stretched out along a minor road, its only focus being its fine out-thrusting thirteenth-century castle. Higher up the valley, near Lampeter, lies the village of Llanybydder, a traditional and current centre of the weaving industry, which is also noted for its horse-trading fairs, a quality of importance in an area infused with pony-lore.

One could, of course, have come down to Cardigan the

other way. Down the breezy, sea-lit coast from Aberaeron
and New Quay. Cardigan, strictly, as county-town of the
previous Mid-Welsh county which borders the bay in Wales's
midriff, and on the northern bank of the Teifi, cannot be
claimed as an element of South Wales. But now that the
single county of Dyfed has merged Pembrokeshire and
Cardiganshire, this small but important town (in Welsh,
Aberteifi) at the river's mouth, can certainly be viewed as one
of the starting points of the south. Cardigan is a busy
shopping town, set interestingly on a hill above the bank of
its tidal river, which — the gleam of stones or the glitter of
water so close to its streets — gives it a slightly salty
character.

To penetrate Pembrokeshire from Cardigan, then, one
simply crosses the bridge, and all the roads are south-flowing,
running into the depths of West Wales. Here, in the lordship
and commote of Cemaes, three chief routes give access to a
very wide variety of interesting features.

Favourites of summer families are the fine bays and
beaches around Newport, which the coastal road makes it its
main business to serve, and which, with their rounded
headlands and their cracked cliffs sheltering a sandy fore-
shore, give a visual interest and a summertime feeling of hot
seas, a backcloth which, visually, few coasts can rival.
Newport itself is, as a village, slightly inland, but extends to
the inlet where the estuary of the river Nevern provides, at
low tide, the wide-stretching beach-ball territory of Newport
Sands. On Carn Ingli, the mountain which overlooks it on the
landward side, is a large hill-fort with hut-circles, of the early
Iron Age. Nearer at hand, on the sand dunes flanking the
Sands, a golf-course provides an outlet for the energies of
fathers who have outgrown their spade-and-sandcastle days.

Like almost every little town in South Wales, Newport has
its castle: originally a twelfth-century Norman baron's
fortress, part of which was modernized for habitation in the
last century. But for historic sites and associations the area as
a whole — the Preseli Mountains and their coastal foothills
— is so full, almost crowded, with interesting items that one
can do little more than wave a brief salute of recognition in
the direction of yet another ruined Norman castle.

Perhaps the most important, and most famous, connection that the Preseli Hills have with pre-history is with that paragon of all our pre-historic monuments, Stonehenge itself. There on the airy, tilting plateau of Salisbury Plain, fragments of Pembrokeshire form, it is reliably concluded, the inner and perhaps most sacred ring of Britain's greatest early monument.

The outer circle of Stonehenge, together with the larger stones of the inner one, is of fairly local origin. These large lumps of sandstone, which were not quarried but found complete and trimmed to the desired size, are to be found still in parts of north Wiltshire, the Marlborough Downs and the area of Newbury. They were probably slid on sledges across the Plain, propelled by manpower. But the bluestones, if indeed they did come from Preseli, had to travel either 150 or 180 miles, at the least, depending on the route. The feat is so improbable, indeed absurd, that it needs a very strong argument to support its likelihood.

This argument was provided in 1923 by Dr H.H. Thomas, who showed that the only part of Britain where all the "foreign" stones present in Stonehenge could have originated was in Pembrokeshire. Indeed the bluestones (those more slender and diminutive pillars which form the inner circle, under the shadow of the great sarsen trilithons) are of a type of rock which does not occur in outcrop form elsewhere in southern Britain. Further researches into Dr Thomas's theory have pinpointed the eastern end of the Preseli Mountains as the likeliest original home of the bluestones. Another foreign stone at Stonehenge, known as the Altar Stone, which is the only one of its kind (micaceous sandstone) in the monument, could have come either from Glamorganshire or from the shores of Milford Haven.

Two questions are left with us by this remarkable theory, and they are questions highly characteristic of Stonehenge in general, which is a traditionally baffling and mysterious construction. How? is one, and Why? is the other.

To deal with the second one first, it seems that the only plausible explanation is that the stones were already holy before they came. It would be hard to imagine a people so obtuse, even in the second millenium B.C., that they would feel it necessary to drag undressed lumps of dolerite and rhyolite more than a hundred miles. Much less hard is it to conceive of a temple to which was already attached a strong tradition of sacredness being moved to form part of an even greater one. It is known now that Stonehenge was radically redesigned about a hundred and fifty years after its original construction; and that it was at this time that the bluestone circle and its associated horseshoe were added. Since they are much less impressive, much less grand, than the great sarsen circle, this cannot have been intended to be any sort of major development or enlargement of the existing structure. The conclusion that there must have been some strong subjective meaning to the addition follows naturally.

The bluestones are not enormous — some in the horseshoe are only about six feet high — but there were originally probably eighty of them; and so it would seem that the answer to the other question (How?) must be: as far as possible by water. Several possible routes have been suggested, the least complex of which is from a departure point near Milford Haven, around the coast of South Wales, and up the Severn Estuary to the mouth of the Bristol Avon, up which they might have been floated for some distance before having to be land-hauled again up onto the plain.

Though in some such way eighty or so bluestones perhaps left the Preseli area, there are plenty of megaliths of comparable antiquity remaining. Among these perhaps the one which is most outstanding, both figuratively and, as it happens, literally, is the splendid chamber-tomb of Pentre Ifan. This, which can be found up a maze of little lanes only thanks to the frequent sign-posts, stands among high fields overlooking the coast and the distant sea. Since the times of early sightseers (it was first described in the sixteenth century), it has been recognized as one of the finest of its type in the country.

There is something about Pentre Ifan which is almost flamboyant, a virtuoso display of skill and inspiration. Though it is built on the same form as many other cromlechs, several of which survive not far away, it is simply larger and grander, and has remained more spectacularly intact. Beautiful and clever, its elegant capstone still confidently in place, it stands out on its breezy slope as a permanent memorial of the values and aspirations of the New Stone Age. Because nobody could have built such a thing without first possessing something more than a mere animal instinct for immediate survival.

There are some signs that this was intended to be only one chamber of a more complex mound, something perhaps in the manner of the great Irish mounds; that Pentre Ifan as it stands might have been the main and central chamber of something more elaborate. Several of the existing uprights form no part of the support of the capstones, forming in fact a crescent-shaped forecourt at the chamber's head. In any case it is a little disappointing to consider that the intention would have been that this piece of immediately apparent skill — its 16-foot long capstone delicately supported on the tips of three 7-foot uprights — would be completely covered over, with earth or pebbles, and never seen at all. In its bare, stripped state it is much more satisfactory than a tumulus, but this effect could not, unfortunately, have been intended.

Stones of later ages, though still distant, abound in the area. Down at Nevern, not far from Newport, the church and churchyard contain a good selection. Nevern is a peaceful little corner of a stream valley, a few cottages loosely connected to the presence of an old bridge and still older church. The latter sits sheltered by an avenue of densely-branched, contorted yews, one of which, known as the Bleeding Yew, adds a bonus to Nevern's already plentiful features of interest. It bleeds agonizingly and for ever, poor yew, a thick magenta blood which oozes from an amputated arm and from a deep wound in its groin to congeal in a sticky river down its side.

Outside the church stands the tall and rich cross of St Brynach (Nevern's dedicatee, a late-fifth-century Irish missionary who is also commemorated at Llanfrynach, Near Brecon). The cross is a fine example of that intertwining, complex patterning so characteristically Celtic and representative of the early Christian period in Ireland and Wales. Subtle, skilful, full rather of motion than of form, it is anything but austere. It can only be intended to delight.

Also at Nevern is the Vitalianus stone, bearing an

inscription in memory of Vitalianus in both Latin and ogam, and another stone similarly inscribed (to Maelog son of Clydai) is set into a windowsill inside. These, together with another also with a dual inscription, the Sagranus stone, in the Parish Church at St Dogmael's (a village on the Teifi estuary downstream from Cardigan), are rare examples in Wales of memorial pillars fairly common on the other side of the Irish Sea. The finest examples of ogam (also sometimes spelt Ogham) are to be found in the National Museum in Dublin, but the Welsh stones are of particular interest because of their bilingual nature.

Ogam is an alphabetic script which consists of lines, representing consonants, and dots, representing vowels. It is, at any rate in its extant form, incised on stones, though there is a theory that an older form of it might have been cut on sticks and used for carrying short messages. The markings are organized around the corner of a pillar, the vowels being indented into the edge itself, and the lines hatched either side or obliquely across it – their position, to right, left, or across, and the number in which they are grouped (from one to five) determining the letter they represent. The inscription commonly runs from the bottom upwards.

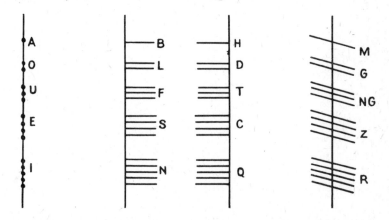

Clearly ogam inscriptions are all very early, some of them, on linguistic grounds, being thought to be of the fourth century; but the form in which they occur makes them difficult to date precisely, and their relation, at any rate as they exist today, to the Latin alphabet, means at least that the form continued well into Christian times. It was the Sagranus stone at St Dogmael's which made it possible, in 1848, for the script (which had somehow become forgotten) to be deciphered.

Today the Preseli Mountains, rising to a modest 1,760 feet, are perhaps best known for their fine views. Northwards you can see, though certainly only on those legendary clear days, the mountains of Snowdonia across Cardigan Bay. Southwards Somerset is sometimes visible, and to the west a lumpy cloud-bank in front of the sunset is, occasionally, the Wicklow Hills. On a normal day the view of the expansive, airy slopes of the mountains themselves is enough, the long sweeps of their green flanks. The turf is springy and thick with vegetation. Wild ponies graze in the tufty grass between the heather patches, and larks scream above them in the light, windy air. To the east afforestation, creeping higher and wider than the scars of the old quarries, has marred the line and texture of those long rolling slopes; the sinuous swell of them and the grain of their fescue and fern are obliterated by the monotone, dimensionless softwoods.

From the hills the Gwaun valley runs down westwards, a wooded valley through which the river Gwaun ripples its way prettily out of the uplands. It flows out at Lower Fishguard, a village of terraced fishing-cottages known, in its own right, as the Cwm, which was once a herring-port and now, in more leisured times, is a busy small-boat sailing centre.

Fishguard — properly called, after its river, Abergwaun — is distinct from the pretty waterside village through which one approaches it. It is defensively placed on top of a fairly steep hill. On the other side of the headland from the lower town is Fishguard's deep-water anchorage and modern harbour, a sheltered bay enclosed by two headlands. On one of these is Fishguard itself, and the town of Goodwick is on the other, facing it across the bay.

Fishguard is a small, not specially attractive place, containing a few old inns and a handful of shops. Vast new developments down at the harbour and on the Goodwick side will gradually shake it out of its backwater life. Hitherto its importance, if that is the word, has been twofold: departure

Pentre Ifan

point of the ferry to southern Ireland; site of the last hostile invasion of Great Britain.

On 22nd February, 1797 an army, or more probably a rabble, consisting of perhaps 600 French infantry and 800 released French convicts, (the numbers vary in different accounts), commanded by the Irish-American General Tate, landed at the cove near Carreg Gwastad Point, a little round the coast from Goodwick. The invasion of West Wales was not, as a matter of fact, intentional. The force was heading for Bristol, where they (probably incorrectly) supposed that support awaited them. A storm, it seems, directed them to the Pembrokeshire coast, where they landed. For some reason (which, like so much else in the story, nobody has ever been able to explain) the ships, having deposited them, departed again at once, leaving the unruly and hungry horde stranded. Lord Cawdor, as Lord Lieutenant of the county, raised the militia, and by noon the next day this efficient force had reacted to the emergency by arriving in the vicinity of the enemy. The latter were, by this time, drunk, having spent the night looting local inns; and there is little doubt that Lord Cawdor's troop of about 750 men was strongly augmented by indignant locals. A rather silly story relates that the Welsh women in their red cloaks were mistaken, by the Frenchmen, for red-coated soldiers, so that the number of the British force surrounding them seemed very much greater than it was. If this were true, which is unlikely, the intoxication of the invaders must have been excessive, and that alone would help to explain why, in spite of their actual superior numbers, they were ready to negotiate with Cawdor that night. Cawdor played his hand strategically, and by 48 hours after the invasion he had won an unconditional surrender. The scene of these negotiations is said to be the Royal Oak Inn, in Fishguard's main square, which bears a proud notice to that effect.

Over beyond Goodwick the country opens out again, to terminate in the high, wave-loud promontory of Strumble Head. To one side of the headland, above the sheltered cove of Pwllderi under its cliffs, is a fine early Iron Age hill-fort, called Garn Fawr. All around the coves of the headland, in certain winds and weathers, grey seals can often be seen. A

Cenarth Bridge

lighthouse on an island broken off from the coastline's tip sits bravely out in the water. Everywhere around the sensory effects are strong, the noise of the seabirds, the sharp fresh wind, the soft grass slopes pitching downwards, the black cliffs and the bright green water.

11   ST DAVID'S

The Pembrokeshire coastline continues its exuberant and breezy display uninterrupted to St David's and round that further corner. It tends to a form very much given to presenting striking views: a headland beyond a headland, the indented, pointed figure of the coastline stretching out in broken progression.

A feature of the rock of this sea-coast is its vulnerability (owing to the joints and cracks in its layered form) to the fissuring impact of waves. Thus, by several stages, the ends of headlands become increasingly isolated; water pounds from either side at the isthmus of rock connecting them, eating deep into it caves which eventually join to leave only an arch. When the arch breaks the tip of the headland is left out on its own, often in the form of a single spiky rock, a feature known as a stack. The same principle leads, in other cases, to such broad, substantial lumps of land as Skomer and Skokholm, Ramsey and Caldy, the inhabitable, grass-topped islands with which the coast of Pembrokeshire is particularly rich.

Visually the result is impressive. There seems to be an island off the end of every headland, an effect which gives to the coastline a thrusting line that forms an approriate expression of its relationship, of attrition and resistance, with the sea.

Most of the islands are now bird sanctuaries, and Ramsey, off St David's, is no exception. Along with the birds the islands sometimes support a number of rodents, more interesting perhaps in that their populations must live, ecologically, in a closed system, and therefore are likely to develop characteristics which eventually cause them to be classified as a sub-species on their own. The island of Skomer, a little to the south, has, for instance, its own vole. Ramsey also has a vole, but this is not sufficiently distinct from the mainland species to be separately classified.

Ramsey island and its associated headland border the north of St Bride's Bay. The town of St David's lies a little inland. The place itself is an unremarkable little city, and has nothing much of interest, in its few small tilted streets, except the great cathedral which lies, remarkably well hidden, just below it.

St David himself chose the site, returning to his home town, then called Menevia, after a period of travelling in England. It was sometime during the first half of the sixth century; David was born around the turn of the century, and almost certainly before 525. The church at Menevia was originally an abbey, a foundation which was to throw a strong influence over Welsh religious life. The site, in this strange hollow under the hill on which the town now stands, can only have been chosen in the hopes that the new buildings would escape the attention of those sea-bandits with which the coast had continually been plagued. It seems that he might as well have set it on a hill, and thus at least chanced the eventual attainment, in Viking-free days, of a building able to display its features more proudly. The abbey in its hollow proved to be insufficiently invisible. The original church was burnt down in 645, and the buildings sacked and destroyed again in 1078 and again in 1088.

David, as abbot of this new monastery, eventually became Bishop of Menevia. Tradition records that he was King Arthur's uncle, and according to Geoffrey of Monmouth (tradition's keenest recorder) he became Archbishop of Caerlon, on the retirement of Dubricius. Many religious leaders of his period are commonly known, by posterity, as saints, a title normally conferred on them unofficially; and it is in fact slightly doubtful that David was ever formally canonized. His biography, an imaginative piece of hagiography, was written in 1090, and is not particularly reliable. Known to the Welsh now and in former times as Dewi Sant, the patron saint was clearly responsible for the founding of many churches throughout Wales, in places where his name is still extant – Capel Dewi, Llanddewi, and so on. He attended the Synod of Brevi, a convention of bishops designed to combat Pelagian heresies, and seems to have made a big impact on his colleagues there, not least by the way in which the ground rose under him when he addressed the gathering, to form a small hill from which he could better be heard. The hill incidentally, is still to be seen, and the church of Llanddewi-brefi (a little north of Lampeter) now stands on it.

David seems to have been a man of determination and dedication, and inspired a Welsh upsurge of Christianity which was mainly responsible for the profusion of 'saints', throughout the country, of the sixth and seventh centuries. He died towards the end of the sixth century, according to Geoffrey of Monmouth dying in his own abbey, which, however, Geoffrey says was founded not by David but by St Patrick. Other authorities are in agreement with him that David was buried there, and in spite of the fact that his remains were removed to Glastonbury in 946 some relics remained at Menevia, which are now stored behind the High Altar.

The supposed canonization of Wales's patron saint took place about 1120, and the cult of St David then spread throughout Wales, to have considerable nationalistic effect during the mid-twelfth century. Pope Callixtus II decreed that two pilgrimages to St David's shrine equalled one to Rome.

The Normans replaced the Welsh as Bishops, at St David's, from 1115 onwards, and the third of these new incumbents, a monk called Peter de Leia, started the construction of the present church in 1180, the old one being, according to the records, 'quite ruinated'. The stone he used came from quarries on the coast immediately to the south-east, two bays in the cliffs of which this Cambrian Sandstone is plentiful. De Leia built the nave, together with the aisles and transepts, and the choir, of the building which we still have. It was badly damaged when the tower fell down in 1220, and again when an earthquake shook it in 1248.

Another Bishop added to de Leia's work during the fourteenth century, increasing the tower by a storey, raising

the height of the walls of the nave, adding Decorated
windows, and putting in the rood screen and the south porch.
   The roof of the nave and the vaulting in the Lady Chapel
belong to the early sixteenth century. The roof lost its lead
during the Civil War, but restorations were carried out in
1696. Nash made some alterations to the west front, which
were reversed in 1863 by Gilbert Scott, who copied a
record of the original design. At that time the whole building
was restored and made secure, fortunately without any
radical attempt to improve its appearance. The result is a
highly individual, very personal building, which still has the
feeling of being very much in use.
   The heavy pink sandstone of the exterior gives little clue
of the Cathedral's real character. It looks solid and serious,
like so many other churches. Inside the soft-grey stone
throws back a fine, pale, chalky light, a blue-greyness which
is strangely, compellingly Celtic, that pale greyness of the
sky, the sea, the stone, the streets, the chimney-smoke and
the tidal sands, which so often fills, soft and pervasive, the
lives of people under the influence of western weather.
   If there is something about St David's interior which is not
quite direct, the effect may be partly attributable to the
angle at which everything tilts. The pillars were thrown out
of the vertical, most probably, by the thirteenth-century
earthquake. The floor fails to achieve the horizontal with less
excuse; there is a drop of 14 feet throughout the whole
building, from east to west, and the nave includes in its
130-foot stretch a three-foot fall. The lean of the pillars, the
slope of the floor, give one immediately, as a quick visual
effect, the feeling that there is something quite different
about this old and solid structure.
   One of the several interesting monuments and tombs in the
cathedral is that of Edmund Tudor, in front of the High Altar
in the centre of the Presbytery. He died in 1456, leaving his
14-year-old wife, already pregnant with the future Tudor
king, in Pembroke Castle, where, in 1457, Henry Tudor was
born. Edmund (who had been created Earl of Richmond by
his half-brother, Henry VI) was buried at the church of Grey
Friars, in Carmarthen. When, in the middle of the following
century, his grandson dissolved the monasteries, Edmund's

remains were transferred to the cathedral, where, appropriately for the father of a dynasty, they occupy an honoured place.

Adjoining the cathedral, over a little stream, the ruins of the Bishop's Palace proclaim, by their grandness, the extreme self-importance of the holders of this high office. The small valley in which the two great buildings sit was called, Giraldus says, the Vale of Roses. "Which ought rather to be named the vale of marble, since it abounds with one, and by no means with the other." It is a mile or so to the coast, where the marble of the chapel came from, and to the little bay called St Non's, where a chapel marks the site of St David's supposed birthplace.

The road, inland of the promontories, strikes the coast again at Solva, as pretty and evocative a place as one could devise. A long deep sheltered creak winds inland, its high banks cutting off any visual connection with the sea, and over it a little village is perched on the hill. The small scale, coupled with the visual enticement of the winding creek, combine to give it its special fascination. It provides good shelter in almost any weather, and has always been, still is, a popular harbour for sailors. Being so small – the miniature fjord and the landing-place beside the Solfach river – it inevitably becomes crowded in the summer. Most beautiful places in the world do; and we should perhaps only be grateful that no municipal authority comes to pack them up and take them away on the last day of September.

The coast road pitches down again, having wandered off the subject, at Newgale, which is little more than a shop and cafe or two amid a great deal of sand. The banked sands stretch impressively on, along the clean side of St Bride's Bay, towards the more complicated country of Broad Haven and Little Haven, an area which belongs more to the other boundary of the Bay. Lanes cobweb the countryside, while the main road sets off inland to do business in Haverfordwest. One can wander endlessly through the details of western Pembrokeshire, and much of the time, unfortunately, do so without seeing anything more than a steep green sloping bank. There is in this area a characteristic, and highly effective form of field-boundary, the purpose of which is not only to keep in the stock but to obstruct the scouring wind.

It takes the shape of a thin A, and appears at first to be made of grass, often being topped by a small thorn edge. In fact it is elaborately built up of interwoven turf and stone, to become a stone wall on which grass grows, the flat top finished off with soil, in which a hedge can be planted if desired, to complete this complex, hybrid structure. The bank-wall thus formed provides a home for primroses, but the most prominent effect quite often is that the motorist spends his time, as in those sunken Somerset lanes, enclosed deeply in a world which stays very much the same.

Doubtless this local feature, which, apart from its slight inconvenience, does much to give the countryside its strongly distinct character, is consciously preserved as part of a planning policy. Because this, these hundred and sixty miles of coastline and occasional inland hilly areas, is a National Park. The Pembrokeshire Coast National Park is not as large as others, (in fact it is the smallest, followed by Exmoor, of the National Parks in England and Wales), but contains, in its highly denticulated, sea-tempered area, probably as dense a concentration of impressive natural scenery, with as few lapses into drabness, as any patch of the country. The park is more or less a coastal strip, only a few miles wide, with two independent inland areas, one of which includes the upper reaches of the Milford Haven waterway – taking in the excellent sailing stretches of the neighbourhood of Lawrenny – and the other the block of upland moors, heath and sheep-farm foothills centred around the Preseli hills, with the softer encroachment of the wooded Gwaun valley.

The Pembrokeshire National Park was created in 1952. It is administered, in the manner of most of the others, by the County Council. Perhaps most notable of its many features is its long-distance footpath, the Pembrokeshire Coast Path.

The Countryside Commission is responsible for the instigation and planning of long-distance paths in Britain, and the subsequent negotiation of agreements, and the administration of the completed paths, is then undertaken by the local authority. Where public rights of way already exist matters are made easier, but in the course of a route stretching over hundreds of miles many new accesses have to be agreed. Consequently of the dozen or so long-distance paths which have been planned, only a few are really continuous for their whole length. Of these the Pembrokeshire Coast Path is the third in length (beaten by the Offa's Dyke Path by one mile, and by the much more famous, high-level walk, the Pennine Way) and was the third to be completed.

It runs for 167 miles, from Amroth on Carmarthen Bay, round the headlands of the Tenby area, up the curling shores of Milford Haven, which must add considerably to its length, to cross (cheating, perhaps?) by ferry from Pembroke Dock to Neyland, continuing through oil-terminal country along the Haven's north shore, round, once again, the mile-making headlands bordering St Bride's Bay to the south, up the long and rather tedious, straight shore of the Bay, past Solva and St David's, over more heady headlands, up the cliff-built, storm-exposed stretch to wild Strumble Head, past Fishguard, Lower Fishguard on the estuary's shore, looping round Dinas Head, down the sandy seasides of Newport Bay, up and over Cemaes Head, collapsing at last, exhausted, down by the Teifi at St Dogmael's, with its ruined Abbey and its ogam stones and its small, stacked, fishing-village streets.

It takes a paragraph to say so, but could take some people several weeks to demonstrate. Fortunately, however, it is perfectly simple to do selected stretches, choosing one's scenery and items of interest, and hopping off at a convenient point, such as, for instance, where the railway strikes the coast at Fishguard. Or doing a length from one of the thoughtfully provided car-parks, to return, the sea-wind on one's other cheek, by the way one went.

The path is by no means consistently spectacular; much of the western end of both shores of the Haven is heavily industrialized, the massive cylinders and belching chimneys of the oil refineries and the power station filling the views; at both Penally and Castlemartin a formidable series of encampments known generally as the Ministry of Defence has completely annexed the territory, and while firing is in progress only the sheep are allowed to risk their self-destruction. The path leaves the coast on these occasions, reluctantly forced inland to wander among the fields. Some stretches, besides, make dull walking, and on many it is of course very unpleasant to be caught by rain; and in one way or another a series of partial walks might seem preferable to the total, courageous undertaking. Nevertheless many parties do it from end to end. There is no doubt whatsoever that it does include, in patches, some of Britain's loveliest coastal scenery. The round green brows of headlands, the black and red spiked rocks below, the bright green water and its white, shooting spray, give, jointly, to St Ann's Head and Stackpole such strong and clear qualities as only equally extreme places elsewhere (the protrusion of a country into an ocean) can offer.

Pembrokeshire is the furthest west piece of Wales, of which, as a country, westernness (with its Atlantic weather and its eroded, escarpmented terrain) is a characteristic. It is surrounded on three sides by sea, so that little of it is more than a few miles inland. The Gulf Stream, in its wanderings, apparently strikes this corner of the Irish Sea's coastline, and, in theory at any rate, makes the sea which lies off those plentiful sandy beaches warmer than most. Sometimes one would hardly think so; but the climate, possibly under the Gulf Stream's influence, is certainly fine and dry, and there are copious statistics to prove it. The lowest winter average is 40 degrees Fahrenheit, and the coastal rainfall, one of Britain's lowest, is 32 inches per year. Both sunshine and wind replace our national murky rainclouds. Hence the sheltering banks which form the field-boundaries, and the angle at which the very few trees which can survive in the salt gales lean their strained branches. The sunshine, however, provides an early season; and one of the most profitable ventures of Pembrokeshire farmers is the new-potato crop, competing with Anglesey to produce the first home-grown potatoes.

West Wales, as the profusion of archaeological remains makes clear, was populated early. The caves were inhabited during the Paleolithic age, and when the ice melted the megalith-builders arrived, with their skill in the handling of giant stones and their knowledge of basic agriculture. The first waves of Celts, metal-workers and fort-builders, arrived during the first millennium B.C., and fortified the promontories and hill-tops with thick-walled, well-built enclosures. The Romans passed by, more concerned with other places, and the Norsemen instead plagued the coast for centuries and left it with many of its characteristic place-names — Grassholm, Skokholm, Gateholm, Skomer, Angle, Dale. It was perhaps the Normans who had the greatest impact of all these waves of invaders, since it was at Pembroke that they sited the hub of that great curve of castles which effectively cordoned off the south of Pembrokeshire from the wild Welsh lands to the north. Within the occupied area everything became Normanized, and the effects to some extent still show. One of the results, in the south of the area, was the introduction of Flemish colonists, to replace the Welsh labour which had been driven out by the imposition of the systems of the new nation. Areas of the south became so completely Flemish by population that the physical appearance of the people even may have been permanently affected.

Until the formation of the new giant county at Dyfed, Pembrokeshire was an administrative unit run from its county town, Haverfordwest. A busy, bustling, traffic-streaming town now, its substantial form and its air of self-importance arise from its location at the junction of all the main roads of the area. Haverfordwest is an old town, a port on the tidal river Cleddau (the Western Cleddau, that is, since an Eastern Cleddau confusingly parallels it, independently, a few miles inland) which flows into, indeed forms, one of the roots of the Milford Haven complex of waterways.

The town, as its layout clearly indicates, is medieval. Besides its function as a port, it formed itself around the lowest bridging-point of the river, in the classical fashion of important towns. The Norman castle now houses a museum, having already undergone considerable changes of use and appearance. It was first built, probably, by the first Earl of Pembroke (whose title, centuries later, Henry VI was to bestow on his Tudor half-brother), Gilbert de Clare, in about the year 1120. The castle formed a useful base for the subordination of West Wales, and king after king made use of it on excursions through the country. Glendower, in 1405, sacked the town below the Castle hill, but the fortress held out. It changed hands twice during the Civil War, and

Cromwell thought it best to remove most of it, finally, in 1648.

> We being authorized by the Parliament to view and consider what garrisons and places of strength are fit to be demolished, and we finding that the Castle of Haverfordwest is not tenable for the service of the State, and yet that it may be possest by ill-affected persons, to the prejudice of the peace of these parts, these are to authorize and require you to summon . . . ye inhabitants of the towne and country of Haverfordwest, and that they forthwith demolish the workes, walls and towers of the said Castle, soe as that the said Castle may not be possesst by the enemy, to the endangering of the peace of these parts . . . If a speedy course be not taken to fulfil the commands of this warrant, I shall be necessitated to consider of settling a garrison.
>
> O. Cromwell.

From what is now left of the old castle, a few lifeless walls, one gets a fair impression of the town. The hilly streets and narrow alleys are densely set, their constriction adding to the busy, crowded character of the place. Among them are several ancient churches, the finest of which, for its clerestories and lancet windows, is St Mary's. The town's most active period, as a port, was perhaps the sixteenth and seventeenth centuries, when it provided a sea link with Bristol, Ireland, and the world by barge and schooner, for the prosperous farming country which forms its hinterland. It had by then acquired the right to hold assizes, and, rather strangely, the privilege of having its own Lord Lieutenant, as if it were a county. In 1853 the South Wales Railway came, to link it to Milford and Carmarthen; and its role as a port began to diminish with the rise of the former. Now, with a population of about nine thousand, it caters for tourism, shopping, commerce, and a good deal of agricultural business.

The coast which forms the northern side of the seaward end of that remarkable stretch of water known generally as Milford Haven, is perhaps one of the most characteristic patches of Pembrokeshire countryside: complicated, sea-surrounded, island-dotted. The shoreline shows the buckle and fold of rock-layers which record events of some hundreds of millions of years ago. Strata are tilted into vertical chimneys, the heaps of broken boulders breaking the line of beach, spectacularly, for instance, at Marloes Sands.

From Little Haven southwards the lanes inland tilt and twist among the banked fields of small farms. Everywhere one is conscious of the long periods of habitation which have influenced and moulded the land. St Bride's and Marloes are small villages now, but archaeological predecessors over-shadow them. An Iron Age fort and a Dark Age settlement at the former, and near the latter, following a similar pattern, a couple of Iron Age promontory forts, and, on the tiny high-tide island of Gateholm, with its views of Skokholm, another Dark Age site.

To the south a further little village, Dale, comes tentatively down to the water, to face the bay known as Dale Roads, where, in sailing days, the larger ships would wait at anchor to be fed by barges coming down the river from Haver-fordwest. The sub-peninsula, flanked by inevitable promon-tory forts to the east and west, sticks out directly southwards to form a sort of protecting spur across the mouth of the Haven. A road goes out to its tip, right to St Ann's Head, that perhaps most vigorous of all these headlands — wild green water, cracked black rocks, rounded grass-slopes falling from blunted plateaux, convexly, to the water.

It was not far from where the lighthouse now is, at the sheltered hollow near the tip of the headland, called Mill Bay, that, early in August 1485, Henry Tudor and his uncle, the Earl of Pembroke, landed with 2,000 men. They had sailed from Harfleur, having been in exile in France since 1470, while the Yorkist monarchy was in power. As the chief Lancastrian heir Henry was in constant danger during this period, and it was only after the successsion of Richard III, whose unpopularity with the nobility seemed to offer a point of weakness, that the Tudors dared to undertake what amounted, in fact, to an invasion. A first attempt had failed, but the Lancastrians were gaining confidence from the course of events in England. Richard, in the meantime, foresaw a possible repeat invasion; and he issued a proclamation which was evidently intended to arouse popular support. "Witness myself at Westminster, the 23rd day of July, in the second year of our Reign . . ."

The said Traitors have chosen to be their Captain one Henry Tydder, son of Edmund Tydder, whom of his ambitions and insatiable covetise encroacheth and usurpeth upon him, the name and title of Royal Estate of this realm of England; whereunto he hath no manner of interest, right, title or colour, as every man knoweth; for he is descended of bastard blood, both on his father's side and of mother's side . . . whereby it evidently appeareth, that no title can or may in him, who fully intended to enter this realm, proposing a conquest, and if he should achieve his false intent and purpose, every man's life, livelihood and goods shall be in his hands, liberty and disposition . . .

Landing at Mill Bay they marched hurriedly north through Wales, gathering supporters on the way. The powerful leaders of South Wales joined them, as they marched from Cardigan into Mid-Wales, and other troops set off from different parts of Wales to meet the Tudors and their growing army in Shropshire. The king in the meantime started north to oppose them, and the two forces met, (Henry with 5,000 against Richard's 13,000), less than three weeks after the landing at Mill Bay, at a small town called Market Bosworth, a little to the west of Leicester.

Marloes Sands, a good bathing beach with, sometimes, sufficient rolling water to make surfing possible, stretches along an unspoilt piece of coast between Westdale Bay and Gateholm. A little further west one can climb through the gorse and bracken to the outlook of Wooltack Point, to gain a view of Skomer, which otherwise is glimpsed only between headlands and over hedges. A flat-topped, sharp-sided, quite extensive island, this, like Skokholm, is a bird-sanctuary, owned by the Nature Conservancy and administered by the West Wales Naturalists' Trust. Visits can be arranged, but are subject, as with all these near-but-far coastal islands, to the weather. And from the headlands, looking out at them, one can sometimes see the spray flowing up their cliffs from the strong swell which protects them, setting them apart from the rest of the land, the territory which has become largely overrun by this one busy species.

More distant, and most inaccessible, of these small patches of rock, is Grassholm, an island eight miles out from Skomer into the Atlantic. It is a gannetry, one of few such places, and is in fact almost entirely covered in gannets. An estimated 15,000 pairs nest there, competing for the limited space with a colony of seals.

Grassholm, the most westerly island of Wales, is identified by scholars with the place called "Gwales in Penfro", which forms the scene of one of the most intriguing passages of the *Mabinogion*, that medieval collection of the remnants of traditional Welsh legend and mythology. The sequence, which occurs in the story of Branwen, has about it a strangely moving element of mystery. Something is being said which we do not quite grasp, but the intensity of feeling behind it comes through to us clearly.

After a disastrous war in Ireland the followers of Bran the Blessed set out with their leader's head to take it to London, where, buried on the White Mount, it would act as a protection for Britain against future invasion. Their journey is imbued throughout with an otherworldly time-scale. They pause at Harlech for seven years, never noticing the passing of time, bewitched by the songs of the birds of Rhiannon. And at the end of that period they set out again for Gwales in Penfro, the next post of their journey.

In the hall in which they took up residence there, a place overlooking the sea, there were three doors. Two of them they found open, and the third, they somehow knew, "that towards Cornwall", it was forbidden them to open and look through.

And notwithstanding all the sorrows they had seen before their eyes, and notwithstanding that they had themselves suffered, there came to them no remembrance either of that or of any sorrow in the world.

This time they stayed for eighty years, unchanging, "nor could any tell from his fellow that it was so long a time." But the stay was at last brought to an end by the impetuous action of one of the troop, who was, eventually, not content with the easy passage of time and the life of comfort which they were experiencing.

This is what Heilyn son of Gwyn did one day. "Shame on my beard," said he, "if I do not open the door to know if that is true which is said concerning it." He opened the door and looked on Cornwall and Aber Henfelen. And when he looked, they were as conscious of every loss they had ever sustained, and of every kinsman and friend they had missed, and of every ill that had come upon them, as if it were even then it had befallen them ... And from that same moment they could not rest, save they set out with the head towards London.

III   MILFORD HAVEN

Ten miles of estuary, sheltered by high banks, and several miles wide, with a minimum low-water depth of eight fathoms. A combination of geographical details makes the harbour of Milford Haven one of Britain's safest natural anchorages. Nevertheless it was slow, in comparison to other ports, to make use of its good fortune. A rural and undeveloped hinterland offered no pressure, and its isolation from the national centres of population and commerce remained unaffected for a long time by new lines of communication. Beyond the fact that Henry II had departed on his invasion of Ireland from there in 1172, history had always been uncharacteristically reluctant to make use of these notable features. Certainly the town had served for a time as a port for Ireland, until the Mail was diverted by Telford's road to Holyhead. A naval dockyard was founded at Milford in 1809, as a response to the possibility of French interest in Ireland. The dockyard closed in 1814, by when the Admiralty had started work on their scheme across the water at Pembroke Dock. And Milford still seemed to be unexpectedly slow in realizing its potential as a port.

Perhaps the town's most famous connection with the Navy and the sea is one which arose from a historical chance in which it was actually only slightly involved, but which it still recalls with apparent pride, in names such as Hamilton Terrace, and the Lord Nelson Hotel. The churchyard at Milford is the burial place of Sir William Hamilton, a local

landowner, who shares with Sir Clifford Chatterley one of
the least enviable claims to fame. Milford Haven was, said
Horatio Nelson, one of the best harbours he had ever seen,
and he must have known many of the world's best ports.
Perhaps it was not every one in which he had a wife (albeit
somebody else's) of Emma Hamilton's calibre.

Nelson and the Hamiltons met in Naples, where Sir William
was the British envoy. Emma was the daughter of a
blacksmith, but appears to have been a woman of great
personal charm. Sir William married her in 1791. And Nelson,
after several apparently hot-headed love affairs, had married,
in 1787, a Mrs Nisbet. His encounter with the Hamiltons
really begins after the Battle of the Nile, in which he was
badly wounded, when he sailed to Naples to refit. Emma
wrote to him before he arrived, in extravagantly enthusiastic
terms, after hearing of the victory. They had met five years
before, when the Captain, as he was then, had been sent to
Naples to raise troops to assist in the siege of Toulon. On this
second visit, however, he stayed some years, and when he
eventually returned to England, in July 1800, it was in the
company of the Hamiltons, with whom from then on he
spent much of his time. He became estranged from his
long-suffering wife a few months later, and the daughter,
Horatia, was born to Lady Hamilton in January 1801.

Sir William had inherited his Welsh estates from his first
wife, and left them to be managed by his nephew and heir,
the Hon. Charles Greville. It was Greville who planned and
built the present town of Milford Haven, into which he
introduced a colony of Quakers, involved in the whaling
business, which had previously been unsuccessfully resident
in Nova Scotia. Sir William seems to have taken a sanguine
and undemanding view of the Nelson affair, and there is no
doubt that he was both fond and pround of Britain's hero.
His only complaint was regarding the expense involved in the
lavish social life which Emma felt necessary. He wrote,
perhaps with mild irony: "I well know the purity of Ld.N's
friendship for Emma and me, and I know how very
uncomfortable it would make his Lp. our best friend, if a
separation should take place." Provided, he said expenses did
not continue to increase, "I am willing to go upon our
present footing."

Manorbier

Nelson's brief period on shore, from 1801 to 1803, included his trip, with the Hamiltons, to South Wales. It was on this occasion that he took an interest, no doubt fostered by Sir William, in Milford Haven.

Nothing transpired, immediatley, from the Admiral's enthusiasm, and Milford's quiet obscurity continued for some time to be uninterrupted. Uninterrupted, that is, except for the unintended arrival, twice, of George IV, who was forced, in 1821, to take refuge there from storms in the Irish Sea. A dirty plaque near the railway bridge commemorates these gracious visits.

Milford Haven now is a scruffy, rather spiritless place, its rundown appearance not at all compatible with its harbour's being Britain's third largest port. Across the water the 250,000 ton tankers, stretching with always unexpectedly prolonged extent against the piers and pipes of the other bank, dwarf all the other, petty, antiquated shipping. And the looming ominous domes and cathedral spires of the refineries and power stations fill the background of the view. Oil refineries occupy much acreage on both sides of the Haven, and in addition oil is pumped from the terminal opposite Milford to refineries at Swansea, sixty miles away. In all, this combined activity has come, by the 1970s, to represent one-third of Britain's oil-refining capacity. The Central Electricity Generating Board have added to the surreal landscape an impressive power-station, oil-fired of course, which is one of the largest of its kind in Europe.

As an oil centre, moreover, the Milford-Pembroke Dock complex has possibly only just begun. Oil drilling in the South Wales sea is opening up previously unimagined possibilities. The boost to Pembrokeshire's economy (estimated at a million pounds for every gusher) which would come about if this operation eventually proves successful, is, of course, turning the heads of some. Others envisage the destruction both of the identity of the community and of the scenic attraction of the coastline. The threat of pollution too, of course, inevitably darkens the horizon.

The Haven has for centuries been crossed by ferry from Neyland, near Milford, to Pembroke Dock. This feature of the area has now suddenly become, like the old Severn ferry,

Carew Castle

an element of the past. An elegant new bridge sweeps across this obvious crossing point, linking the important industrial complexes of the two sides of the Cleddau estuary.

Pembroke Dock and Pembroke are very close together, but they are completely different places. The Dock, down by the Haven, has an ordered, unspontaneous appearance and an atmosphere of planned correctness. The streets are too wide and too straight to have come into being by a natural process, and the severe regularity with which the town is laid out makes it a place which would be, one feels, a little hard to live in. Moreover it is dominated by the aggressively barrack-like wall of the dockyard, the general area of which is now turned over to largely industrial use.

Pembroke Dock was built by the Admiralty in 1814, following a decision not to renew the lease on the Milford Haven dockyard. The construction of the town followed that of the dockyard, and it was indeed laid out on an almost military basis, like a Roman camp. Strangely the buildings themselves (as opposed to their totality) do not look like part of such a rigorous plan, since they are mostly those little terrace cottages of nineteenth-century Wales, well-built and with slight variations of detail, climbing the steep hills, running along the slopes, everywhere neat and respectable. What the place amounts to now, most of all, is a fine display of nineteenth-century domestic architecture and town planning.

Over the hill one pitches into Pembroke itself unexpec-tedly. Suddenly you are crossing the Pembroke River, and it is there. There is the familiar stretch of the castle walls with the fat central tower, and at their feet, strangely small and unimpressive, the jumbled, lively town.

The province of Penbroch adjoins the southern part of the territory of Ros, and is separated from it by an arm of the sea. Its principal city, and the metropolis of Demetia, is situated on an oblong rocky eminence, extending with two branches from Milford Haven, from whence it derived the name of Penbroch, which signifies the head of the aestuary.

It is uncharacteristic of Giraldus to be so factual and as it

happens, after an outline of the history of the castle up to his
day, he then digresses to relate the strange behaviour of some
weasels and to give descriptions of a local species of unclean
spirit which had made a habit of throwing dirt at people,
"more with a view of mockery than of injury".

A broad band of castles runs, by no coincidence, in a loop
around Pembroke, its boundary forming a division between
the country which the Normans had settled and brought
under their laws, and the rest of West Wales in which the
Welsh were still allowed, reluctantly, to keep their way of
life. Within the strip – eight to fourteen miles wide – the
imported Flemish population, brought in during the reign of
Henry I, worked on the manors in the place of the ousted
Welsh. And the remains of this colonization today take the
form of a concentration of great houses and castles in the
southern part of the county, and, as a possible distant result,
the clustering in the area of predominantly English-speaking
communities. The effect on Pembrokeshire has been permanent also in the form of a traditional division between north
and south, the two halves of the former county continuing to
regard themselves as almost separate realms.

Pembroke is an old town; the Normans moved swiftly into
South Wales, and Henry I had evidently considered it worthy
of a charter even before the end of the eleventh century. The
town and its castle are built on a limestone ridge – Giraldus's
'oblong rocky eminence' – on the bank of the Pembroke
River at the point just before it widens to become yet
another bay of the Haven. Doubtless there were fortresses of
a sort there before the Conquest, but the practice of erecting
large-scale stone-built castles was one which was new to
Britain. William the Conquerer came to Pembrokeshire
himself in 1081, and during the next decade the construction
of the present castle probably began. The castle then passed
into the hands of the powerful nobility, whose position was
eventually formalized, in 1138, by the creation of the
Earldom of Pembroke. The first earl, Gilbert de Clare, was
nicknamed Strongbow, and became the archetype of those
semi-autonomous Marcher Lords with whom the Crown
maintained, for centuries, a precarious *modus vivendi*.

Because of the might and independence of the earls,

Pembroke and its area retained a considerable amount of separate identity, being almost a miniature English kingdom, well into the sixteenth century. The earls held their own Courts, imposed their own laws, administered their domain financially as well as judicially, with their own Exchequer and Court of Chancery. It was under these conditions that Pembroke Castle grew.

The first Strongbow, Gilbert de Clare, was probably only responsible for a small amount of the increase in size. He was succeeded by his son Richard, who, having married into the Irish royal family, set about subduing Ireland, using Pembroke as a base. Henry II (who was to continue the Irish wars which Strongbow had started) visited the Castle in 1172, on his way to sail to Ireland from Milford Haven. Richard Strongbow died four years later, and for a time (since he had no heir except a small daughter) the castle reverted to the king. He let it go again eventually, by marrying the girl, with her possessions, to William Marshall, who thus became Earl of Pembroke, in 1189. The Marshall family remained in residence until 1245, and it was probably during this period that the Great Keep and the main Hall (the 'Norman Hall') were constructed.

During the thirteenth century there were frequent outbreaks of trouble both in Wales and in Britain as a whole. The Marshall family came and went, the last of William's five sons dying (as did they all) childless, so that, in 1245, the property then passed to a daughter and, by her marriage, into another family. The castle received extensions again, and, during a period of peace, such impressive features as the Northern Hall were probably built. It was not until 1389 that the new family in turn finally petered out, and the earldom, together with the castle, reverted to the king, who was at that time Richard II.

By then Pembroke had assumed almost its complete form, the complicated amalgam of additions by two main families over at least two centuries, which has made it one of the largest castles in the country.

Bolingbroke revived the earldom in 1399, after he had, by forcing Richard's abdication, become Henry IV; but it lapsed again in the reign of his grandson, in 1447. And thus the title was available when, in 1453, Henry VI decided that it would be politic to recognize the existence of his Tudor step-brothers.

The Tudors were an old Anglesey family originally, respectable, land-owning, and even perhaps, in a regional way, distinguished. Had it not been for a series of improbable chance events, they might have remained no more than local officials and dignitaries with some amount of influence in North Wales. They traced their descent to Ednyfed Vychan, lieutenant to Llewelyn the Great. As kinsmen of Glendower, they fought in support of his rebellion. And Owen Tudor, finally, left Anglesey to go to war with the troops of Henry V, in France.

Owen no doubt fought at Agincourt, and it is possibly as a result of distinguished conduct there that he found himself, after the king's early death, clerk of the wardrobe in the Queen's Household. The widowed queen, still aged only 21, was herself the daughter of a king of France, Charles VI – Catherine de Valois, mother of the infant king, Henry VI. At what stage she and Owen Tudor had started their affair we do not (much as we should like to) know. It is remarkable but almost certain that, after the king's death, they illegally and dangerously got married. During the next fourteen years, for which the secret was kept, the marriage produced three Tudor sons. Such secrets, though, cannot be kept for ever, and when it broke, in 1436, the Queen-dowager retired to a nunnery, in which she died the next year. Owen was called before the Council and arrested, consequently being sent to Newgate, from where he twice escaped. In 1439 the king found him becoming too much of an embarrassment, and sent him home to Anglesey.

Owen Tudor, as a staunch Lancastrian, lived to fight on, and was inevitably involved in the Wars of the Roses, which raged throughout the subsequent period. Finally at the battle of Mortimer's Cross the Yorkists won a critical victory, and Owen, then aged 76, was executed at Hereford, a sad and undistinguished end for the husband of a queen and grand-father of a king.

Henry VI, in the meantime, had bestowed his official recognition on the liaison, by granting to his Tudor half-

brothers their earldoms. Edmund, the eldest, was created Earl
of Richmond, and a marriage was arranged with Margaret
Beaufort, the Duke of Somerset's daughter. It was through
her that the Tudor family became the heirs to the House of
Lancaster, since her grandfather, John Beaufort, Earl of
Somerset, was (like Henry Bolingbroke) a son of John of
Gaunt, the Duke of Lancaster.

Jasper Tudor, the second son, became the Earl of
Pembroke. He moved into Pembroke Castle, and continued
the work of his predecessors in adding architectural features
to his home. Edmund, the Earl of Richmond, Jasper's elder
brother, was at the time (like his father) fighting in the Wars
of the Roses, and had placed his child-wife, Margaret, then
aged only 14 but already pregnant, under the care of his
brother in Pembroke Castle. He died at Pembroke in 1456,
and shortly afterwards the child was born there, born Earl of
Richmond and, through his prominent position in the House
of Lancaster, immediately a dangerous rival to the Yorkist
faction, which finally gained the throne in 1461.

Leland was in Wales during the 1530s, that is, during the
reign of the son of the man we are concerned with, and
claimed to have seen the room then identified as being the
one in which the girl Margaret gave birth to Henry Tudor.

> In the Outer Ward I saw the chamber where King Henry VII was
> borne, in knowledge whereof a chymney is new made with the
> armes and badges of King Henri.

This is now thought to be a first-storey room in the nearest
tower to the Gatehouse, which is called now the Henry VII
Tower. The evidence is slight, and it seems that it may just as
well have been in some other room of the then many-roomed
castle that the significant event took place.

The boy remained at Pembroke, under the care of his
uncle (who was to continue his influence and attention
throughout his career until he gained the throne) until, in
1470, the defeat at Tewkesbury and an attack on the castle
made it seem wise to withdraw to a safer distance. From
Tenby Jasper Tudor and his young nephew sailed to Brittany,
where they lived in constant danger of betrayal for the next

15 years. Several times the Yorkists tried to bribe the Duke of Brittany to hand over their dangerous rival, and on one occasion they almost succeeded. Finally, on the death of Edward IV and succession of Richard III, a period at which the nobility, distrusting the new king, were fleeing to France, it seemed that the time had come to launch an invasion.

Jasper became Earl of Pembroke again, having lost the title during his exile, and when he died the Earldom returned to the king, then Henry VII, who was in any case his natural heir. He in turn conferred it on his son, and he, Henry VIII, retained it for the throne. Anne Boleyn was given the title of Marchioness of Pembroke, in 1532. James I gave the castle to one of his subjects, and in 1642 it was defended for Parliament against the Crown.

In a predominantly Royalist area it was remarkable that the fortress was then able to withstand sieges and attacks until 1645. When, in 1648, the fighting having largely finished, Cromwell thanked the men who had held Pembroke throughout the first stage of the war, and ordered them now to disband, they, with that almost manic independence of central authority which had always characterized the town of Pembroke, refused to do so. It seems to us now that it was also with not a little irrationality that the holders of Pembroke, Rowland Laugharne and Colonel Poyer, then refortified the castle and prepared for another war. When the area was Royalist and the king was winning they were Parliamentarians. Now, over-reacting to Cromwell's supposed insults, they became Royalist, at the very moment when the king's cause was almost lost.

It seemed for a time that what was happening was in fact a second revolution, the frequent result of the success of an initial one. The result might well have been a universal uprising against Cromwell, and, not surprisingly, he took quick and forceful action to stop it. He came to Pembroke himself in May 1648, and for eight weeks besieged the town. The castle's enormous strength was then thoroughly tested, as Cromwell sent for more artillery and ammunition. Attempts to scale the walls failed, and it seemed that the only way to oust the garrison was to wait for them to starve.

Nobody came from the rest of war-torn Britain to help them, and in the second week of July, their food and water almost finished, the stubborn garrison surrendered.

It was Cromwell's provident policy to destroy wherever he could the fortresses which he had had trouble in taking, knowing as he did that trouble is hardly likely to come to a sudden end, and having the sense to take this precaution against a repeat of the same difficulties. As a result many of the walls of Pembroke fell, but so strong were other parts that Cromwell's powder had little effect on them. The Barbican Tower, for instance, near the Gatehouse, was only badly shaken by the explosion, the force of which lifted its domed roof but failed to break it. The Great Keep itself, that round, plain, central feature, the sturdiness and medieval dogmatism of which gives to Pembroke much of its strength of character, probably seemed to him too hopeless a task even to attempt. The walls are 14 feet thick, at the base over 19, and made of large undressed blocks of local limestone. It was built by either the Strongbows or the Marshalls, in the early days of the castle's use as a fortress, and must have formed the main defensive base and lookout post of the nucleus which then existed of today's rambling complex.

Pembroke Castle was neglected from then on, Cromwell's destruction of what he could of it having left it useless as a habitation, and restorations took place in the 1880s and the late 1920s. Unlike most of the bigger castles it did not pass, during the first half of this century, into the control of the Ministry of Works (or, as they are at present called, the Department of the Environment), and in modern times has remained under the care of Pembroke Borough Council.

To some extent the grand and imposing exterior of Pembroke Castle, which it owes to its exceptional size and its fortunate position, is in contrast to the slightly chaotic, uncohesive mixture of buildings and partial buildings inside. The interior suffers from its being a hotch-potch of renovations, themselves imposed on the considerable variety of its original styles. The rebuildings and restorations, being carried out by different people at widely different periods, have followed no clear pattern, so that one finds, for instance, windowless rooms which have evidently been intended, with

their new floors and central heating, to be in modern use. But
the outside of the building is superb, a grand and beautiful
military edifice fully worthy of its one-time importance.

One feature which Pembroke Castle has which certainly
distinguishes it, is that huge natural cave under its foundations, called the Wogan. One comes down to it out of the
Northern Hall by a small, dark, endless spiral staircase. The
journey in the darkness adds, perhaps, to the other-world
appearance of the place into which one emerges. It is difficult
to know quite what one would expect, coming out from this
dizzy descent into the quiet light which the Wogan draws
from its opening onto the river bank, but the effect is always
slightly surprising, slightly unreal. It is large, some 80 to 90
feet one way by 50 to 60 the other, roughly shaped, or
shapeless, with a high, almost vaulted roof. It seems, in the
poor light, to be full of mysterious dark corners. It drips, and
echoes to the slightest noise. Most, perhaps, it is conspicuously empty, a huge vacant hole in the rock, a stange,
lofty, underground pocket of nothing.

On this south side of the Haven the oil refineries and their
associated works stretch as far as Angle Bay. The little town
of Angle itself, however, remains as rural as ever, lying in its
hollow between two shores. On the seaward side the coast is
open and varied, providing plentiful sandy beaches. West
Angle Bay is typical, and Freshwater West one of the largest
and most scenic, although the bathing is unfortunately not
always safe. Above the strand, on the dunes, stands the
chamber-tomb known as the Devil's Quoit.

The sinister area of the Castlemartin and other firing
ranges blocks off much of this southern stretch of coastline,
grim notices and unequivocal fences threatening peril and
punishment, and reminding us uncomfortably that some
people, at any rate, do not consider that the world has
entered a state of permanent peace. But a corner of this lump
of country is still accessible, in the neighbourhood of
Bosherston, where one unexpectedly encounters an area of
lushly treed, tropical-looking country. Old timber and tall
bushes around swampy hollows.

Bosherston lakes form a three-mile stretch of fresh water
which now provides in almost equal proportion fish (mainly

pike) and water lilies. Through this area one can penetrate to the coast, and, when the tanks and other armaments are not firing, even drive nervously through the military ranges to the headlands.

Much of the striking nature of the coastline, all through Pembrokeshire, is derived directly from its rocks. In many places, as around this area of St Govan's, the carboniferous limestone and the Old Red Sandstone coincide. Throughout the coastal country one gets, on land, the strange effect of bright maroon fields, formed of soil crumbled from the red stone; and on the seashore, where the sandstone has worn away, the stacks and caves, and great blocks of boulders, formed by the limestone. It makes it, visually, a constantly amazing and unreal coast.

Perhaps this effect is best typified at St Govan's, where, in the cove to the west of the headland, the saint's tiny chapel stands. It stands jammed into a ravine, half-way down a slope, and whoever St Govan was he would have needed a good reason (lost to us, like much else about him) for sticking it there. The Authorities, though never failing to give a confident opinion, differ radically about who this Govan was. He was the Arthurian Gawaine, having become a hermit, state some. He was, on the contrary, a woman, others declare — Cofen, the legendary wife of a local king. However elusive his (or her) identity may be, the chapel is solid and indisputable enough. The path runs down into it and passes through, to continue down the cliff the other side. An old stone altar, sometimes, rather fancifully, said to be the tomb of Govan, is the only feature in the main part of the cell. Through an arch to the side of it one enters an even smaller room, where a cleft in the rock is supposed to have opened to conceal the saint when persecuting pagans were pursuing him (or her). There is (it is that sort of place) a tradition that one cannot count the steps descending to the chapel and get the same result when counting them again on the way back up. There are (investigation reveals) between 71 and 73 of them, and this rather puzzling fact perhaps depends on whether one counts the treds of the rises. And yet such an attempt to account for the discrepancy seems somehow shallow and weak-willed. The effect is most probably due to magic.

Below the chapel breaks the sea, crashing up and inwards among those immense blocks. One crawls, dwarfed, over and among them, under the arches of free-standing buttresses, below the dangerously towering pinnacles which, one day during these next few thousand years, must eventually capitulate to the attrition of one last onslaught, and collapse in monstrous fragments to add more massively tumbled blocks to the chaos on the shore.

A bay with a very different character, further east on the same stretch of coastline, is the small sheltered inlet of Manorbier. Here the Old Red Sandstone reaches down to the beach, and a fault in it provides a nest for the small valley with its stream. On the beach itself the rock lies tilted, its curious ridges stretching down the shoreline like the lines of ploughing. As in so many cases, it is the geological conformation of the place which, initially, gives it its strange attraction.

Manor-beer it is pronounced, a name derived perhaps from the word Pyrr, a plural meaning 'lords'. Or perhaps not. The etymology of the unusual name is only a matter of conjecture. The castle itself, however, is well enough recorded, a fine ruin on a small hill, which, when it was new in the reign of Henry II, must have looked well worthy of the praise which Giraldus understandably lavished on it. It was the seat of the de Barri family, and it was there, in probably 1147, that Giraldus himself was born.

Demetia, therefore, with its seven cantreds, is the most beautiful, as well as the most powerful district of Wales; Penbroch, the finest part of the province of Demetia; and the place I have just described, the most delightful part of Penbroch. It is evident, therefore, that Maenor Pirr is the pleasantest spot in Wales; and the author may be pardoned for having thus extolled his native soil, his genial territory, with a profusion of praise and admiration.

Giraldus, or Gerald de Barri, was the son of a Norman lord with extensive South Wales possessions, who took his family name from Barry Island on the extreme south coast of Glamorgan. Gerald's mother was the daughter of Gerald de Windsor, her mother, in turn, being the daughter of Rhys ap Tewdwr Mawr: none other than the Princess Nest, a woman

of legendary beauty and attraction, who, after an affair with
Henry I, had been given in marriage to de Windsor, with
consequent stormy results in South Wales for years to come.
Through this connection Gerald de Barri was a cousin to the
Lord Rhys, whose power in South Wales during his time
almost amounted to that of a monarch.

Gerald studied in Paris, and on his return set out on a
promising career in the church. By the age of 21 he was
Archdeacon of Brecon. And in 1183, no doubt as a result of
his connections of kinship, he found himself negotiating with
the Lord Rhys, after the latter's continued rebellion, to
arbitrate a settlement with the king. During the reign of
Henry I the kingdom of Deheubarth had been annexed by
the Normans and split up into manors. His death in 1135 led
to outbreaks of fighting in South Wales, with the result that
many of the lordships were defeated and the kingdom, in
effect, restored. During the reign of Stephen chaos continued, so that the situation which Henry II found in 1154,
when he succeeded to the throne, was far from satisfactory
from the English point of view.

From 1158 to 1163 Henry continued to attempt to
retrieve for the Normans the lands then held by Rhys ap
Gruffydd of Deheubarth, who was directly descended from
the line of Welsh princes, including such great rulers as Hywel
Dda and Rhodri Mawr. Finally the king admitted the power
of the hereditary ruler of South Wales to the extent of
allowing him freedom of rule over his traditional kingdom,
though it had been agreed that his title was to be that of
Lord. From his seat at Dinefwr Castle, near Llandeilo, he
ruled a larger and more stable kingdom than even some of his
ancestors had succeeded in doing in the days of independence.

Perhaps as a result of carrying out this tricky job, Gerald
was then appointed, in 1184, Court Chaplain to the king. He
went with the young Prince John to Ireland in 1185, and as a
result then wrote his *Topography of Ireland*. In 1188 he set
out again, on that famous and, for us, fortunate tour of
Wales, with Archbishop Baldwin, to recruit and fund-raise for
the Third Crusade.

Baldwin spent his time in Wales preaching, and Gerald,

evidently, talking, listening, and making notes. The resulting *Itinerary* is largely a collection of local legends, showing both avid interest and great credulity. The *Itinerary* is followed by a shorter *Description of Wales*, which, part factual and part fanciful, gives both wildly mistaken information and some fascinating details of first-hand observation. The people, he describes as "light and active, hardy rather than strong", and almost entirely living on the produce of their own farming. Both sexes wear short hair-cuts, "close round to the ears and eyes", and take great care of their teeth "by constantly rubbing them with green hazel and wiping with a woollen cloth". Being "of a sharp and acute intellect" they excel in any studies they undertake. They are also highly musical and witty. He notes their lack of class-based subservience, and wonders why it is that the English have always lacked this facility; the English also "still retain the exterior fairness of complexion and inward coldness of disposition" whereas the Welsh have a "natural warmth of temper from which their confidence is derived". It cannot, he concludes, be due to the climate.

With great fairness he also catalogues the population's faults, and must to some extent take the blame for founding the stereotype image of the fickle Welshman. "These people are no less light in mind than in body, and are by no means to be relied upon." They are "constant only in inconstancy". They are too fond, he says, of intoxicating drink, much given to the crime of incest, and quarrelsome.

It is all written in a highly personal, buoyant style, and records for us many intimate details of medieval Wales which no chronicle, history or learned study would ever do. It appears that Wales was then a strange mixture of the noble and the absurd, a sort of small-scale symposium of social idioms and eccentricities.

There is something of this individuality of character remaining in the little valley of Manorbier, a valley of considerable charm, with its streams and sandy bay, its tall-towered church, and, set on the slope across from the church in such a way that the two form appropriate principal features, its castle. Manorbier castle has retained the infor-mal, unofficial feeling shared to some degree by many of the

Pembrokeshire castles, which have escaped the rigorous and standardizing rehabilitation imposed by the Ministry of Works. It still feels very much like somebody's home.

Another castle which contains, at the same time, those qualities of grandness and intimacy, is only about four miles away, at Carew. It faces onto the water on the other side of what is virtually a long narrow peninsula, at the shore of one of the extreme branches of the Milford Haven waters, where the Carew river comes down to join the Cresswell, the two combining at Lawrenny to give a fine expanse of sheltered inland tidal stretches, a yachting and boating area comparable to the Norfolk Broads.

Carew Castle, still romantically ivied, and, at high-tide, effectively reflected in the river at its feet, sits alone on its tidal inlet. The whole nature of the place, in fact, is tidal, the scenery being affected radically by that daily filling and withdrawing. There is, to emphasize the point, a Tide Mill, a little way downstream, at which, until not long ago and from the early seventeenth century, the dam caught the waters which had flooded in to use the gathered power of their outflow for the grinding of corn.

This castle was perhaps built by Gerald de Windsor, on the site of an earlier one, when, by his marriage to Princess Nest, he acquired property in the area. As it stands now, however, much of it is of later date, though the main structure of the outside is from late in the thirteenth century. Rhys ap Thomas, whose forces swelled the army which Henry Tudor brought with him when he landed in the Haven, built a substantial part of the interior during the years succeeding Bosworth. Rhys, as the current head of the Dinefwr family, the heir to the Princes of Deheubarth, contributed not only his spearmen but his influence to the success of Henry's attempt on the throne. The castle took a further, more elaborate form, under the hands of Sir John Perrot, in the next century, when the north side of it was virtually converted into an Elizabethan country house.

Not far from the castle and the mill stands Carew's other exhibit, a fine wheel-cross of early date, displaying that intricate and flowing line which is so characteristically Celtic. This and the other Pembrokeshire one at Nevern are perhaps two of the best examples of the form. The Carew one bears an inscription thought to refer to the Welsh king Maredudd, who died in 1035.

This south corner of West Wales is rich in many things, in beach-sand, in megaliths, castles, sunshine and sandstone. It seems almost unfair that it should also have acquired, somehow, one of Britain's best small resorts.

Tenby is on a headland, one result of which is that it is initially a rather confusing place. It seems that whichever direction one walks in one encounters the sea. Another result, however, is that it has a choice of beaches, and consequently, in an area where the warmth of the climate is only tempered by the constancy of the sea-wind, the opportunity, almost always, to find shelter. It is, quite unlike most resorts, stuck up high above the beach, with little or no points at which the town and the sea actually converge. Inconvenient as this may be for those who tend to run short of energy or breath, it gives the place a dramatic and individual nature, lavish with striking views both of itself (the houses and hotels on the brinks of cliffs, the contrast of the wide flat sands with the vertical, serrated aspects of the rocks and town) and, distantly across Carmarthen Bay, of the hills and headlands of Gower.

In addition to this general prominence, Tenby adds some further scenic masterstrokes to its altogether almost stagey display. The Castle Hill, a rock between the two main aspects of the town – the harbour and the beach – which continues the line of the headland into the sea, juts into the view from many parts of the town. Beyond it again, perched in the sand or sea of a scene-changing tide, is St Catherine's Island, a cliff-path veering up from its access across the sand to the formidable retreat (which has served many purposes, and lately that of a zoo) on its rocky summit.

Finally there is Caldy Island; and even Tenby, with its extensive views of sand-dunes and coastline, and its high, sea-filled, breezy outlook, would be less scenically superb without this beautiful piece of land in the sea. The island is inhabited and run by Cistercian monks, who, besides their traditional craft and trade of distilling perfumes from the local flowers, get much involved, in the summer, in the

tourist business. *Tempora mutantur, nos et mutamur in illis.*
Boat trips run from the harbour in fine weather, either for
the day to Caldy or around it and its offshoot, St Margaret's
Island, to view the seals and seabirds. Caldy meanwhile, in all
weathers and seasons, provides that incomparable view from
the Esplanade, and adds considerably to the excitement of
approaching Tenby down the coast.

Though much of the town, respectable resort that it is, has
that air of Victorian watering-place which pervades the
sea-fronts of Aberystwyth and Llandudno (not to mention
Eastbourne and Brighton), the place is, in fact, extremely
old. The Town Walls still at least partly close off the
headland on which the old town, with its castle and harbour,
stands. One enters this quarter through a gateway in the wall,
a fact which always, as in Yugoslavian and Cretan Venetian-
empire towns, impresses a consciousness of enclosure, consolidation, and well-established identity. A town within a
wall cannot sprawl, clumsily or carelessly, unaware of its
nuclear focus. Nor can it waste space with anti-social
pretensions to dominance by any of its occupants. The Tudor
Merchant's House, clearly a product of prosperity, sits
jammed among its neighbours of later centuries with a
small-town recognition of equality. Narrow streets get bent
out of course, with the result of quickly-changing vistas
constantly revealing small, framed, snapshot views of jumbled
angles and facets.

Though not much remains of it, the castle originated in the
early thirteenth century. Tenby came into prominence and
prosperity during the Middle Ages (a poem, dated at not later
than 1200, recounts its fame), and its framework, centred on
the harbour, together with its walled character and pattern of
narrow streets, belong to its successful period of the
fourteenth and fifteenth centuries. The Tudor Merchant's
House (which was given by the Corporation to the National
Trust in 1937) is of the late fifteenth or early sixteenth
century, and gives a clear idea of what sort of place the town
was then. Another early fifteenth century house is next door,
and possesses a good example of a Flemish chimney.

Henry IV had, by then, given the town a charter, and its
trading importance continued (with both an export trade to

Pembroke Castle

France and Spain and an internal connection with Bristol and elsewhere in Britain) until the sixteenth century. The walls, which had been partly renewed in 1457, were strengthened again in anticipation of the Armada. By the eighteenth century the commercial importance of the town had decreased, but it came to life again in the nineteenth as the sort of pleasant, mild-weathered leisured place which it is today.

If one can isolate from among the town's consistent charms one aspect in which it excels most noticeably, it must be the wide, clear stretch of the South Beach below it. Under the cliffs and stacked hotels of the Esplanade the sands stretch, when the big tide withdraws, unobstructed from the rock's foot to the waves' edge, a mile and a half from Castle Hill to Giltar Point, their surface clean and level, bright with fragments of oyster-shell and mussel, out beyond the presence of the town, past Golf Course sand-hills, with adequate expanse, thank goodness, for the significant proportion of this beach-loving nation which they periodically attract. In the winter though one can walk them alone, alone except for the black dots of a woman and a dog along the distant rocks, and the single line of one's own footprints marking a progress towards no clear conclusion across an otherwise undifferentiated field of bright dry sand.

Saundersfoot does for Tenby now what Rhyl does (in a cruder way) for Llandudno; it relieves the pressure. People who loved it as it was inevitably feel regret, seeing the way the new buildings dominate the waterfront there and the activities of a noisier world overwhelm the peaceful and pretty place-on-the-beach which it once was. But somewhere there has to be provided room for the Bingo and the discothèques, since the need for them is as real and pressing as any other need, and we must only be glad that these influences have not yet swept through Tenby. With the growth of the popularity of yachting, the harbour at Tenby, too, has become unequal to the pressure, and is saved from expansion by the use by yacht associations of the quays and moorings of Saundersfoot.

The anthracite coal belt comes to an end on the shore at Saundersfoot, where an exposed anticline of it can actually be seen, the last outpost of that rich and important belt

Dylan Thomas's shed
The Boat House, Laugharne

which stretches from the Tawe valley west and from
Ammanford southwards into the water of Carmarthen Bay.
The origin of the town, through its harbour, is due to the
success of the coal trade, though this industrial background
has now completely disappeared. Sea-fishing and boat-
tripping supplement yachting, to keep the town busy during
the summer; and its long sandy beach absorbs some of the
many people who flood into the town. Beaches play a large
part in the countryside's make-up from Saundersfoot onwards, where the coastline itself becomes gentler and less
visually striking. Wiseman's Bridge and Amroth, still small
and relatively quiet, are basically villages on the beach. The
latter (where the long-distance footpath sets out on its
daunting way) has as its most famous feature a submerged
forest, which, however, spends the greater part of its time, as
indeed submerged forests should, under the opaque, reflec-
tive sea.

Sand there is, though, plentifully, sand stretching for miles
and miles, towards Pendine and even bigger beaches, towards
Laugharne Burrows and even greater quantities of sand.

IV   CARMARTHEN

Though Pembrokeshire is pre-eminently coastal, a road comes
through it inland, from Cardigan to Tenby, cutting through
the districts, skirting the Preseli Mountains, running through
stable farming country, out of sight of the sea. A time-shift
shakes us again at Narberth, its jolt briefly rattling the bones
of the values and qualities of the ages which have intervened
between the cromlechs and the oil-tankers. Nothing about
South Wales, for all its patches of superficial squalor and its
dominant air of economic strain, is really new, the country
having been inhabited as long and as continuously as most
areas of Europe. It would be inappropriate, for instance, to
try to pass through this area of camps and castles without
considering the location of the court of Pwyll prince of
Dyfed.

The *Mabinogion* opens with the words "Pwyll prince of Dyfed was lord over the seven cantrefs of Dyfed; and once upon a time he was at Arberth, a chief court of his . . ." His court at Arberth recurs, throughout the two stories concerned with him, which have their setting in South Wales. But never so appealingly as when, after a feast, he went out of the court to sit on Gorsedd Arberth, a mound which was above it. He was informed that the mound had this peculiarity: whatever high-born man sat on it, he would not leave it without either suffering injuries or seeing a wonder. Pwyll did not fear, he told his followers, that he would receive wounds in the company of such a host. "But as to the wonder, I should be glad to see that."

As he and his companions sat there, "they could see a lady on a big fine pale white horse, with a garment of shining gold brocaded silk upon her, coming along the highway that led past the mound." The rider passed slowly, and the prince sent a man to find out who she was. On foot he could not catch up with her, and Pwyll sent him back to the court to fetch the fastest horse.

> He took the horse and off he went. He came to the open level plain and showed his horse his spurs; and the more he pricked on his horse, all the further was she from him. Yet she held to the same pace as that she had started with.

The messenger came back, defeated. Puzzled by the occurrence, they all went back to the court. The next day, after their meal, they went again to sit on the mound, this time taking with them the fastest horse they could find. In a short time the same lady came past, dressed as before, slowly riding her horse down the road which passed the mound. The prince's man prepares to ride after her, but at once she has gone past.

> Yet her pace was no mure hurried than the day before. Then he put his horse into an amble, and thought that despite the easy pace at which his horse went he would overtake her; but that availed him not. He gave his horse the reins; even then he was no nearer to her than if he went at a walking pace.

Once again he gave up and came back; and they all went back into the court. The next day, the third and crucial time, they went to watch again. Pwyll himself on this occasion had his own horse prepared, and when the rider appeared he mounted. For some time he rode after her, "and he thought that at the second bound or the third he would come up with her. But he was no nearer to her than before." He then, for the first time, decided to speak.

> "Maiden," said he, "for his sake whom thou lovest best, stay for me." "I will gladly," said she, "and it had been better for the horse hadst thou asked for this long since."

It is, it turns out, Rhiannon, who will, after some further difficulties, become Pwyll's wife. Horses, as a theme, accompany her throughout her *Mabinogion* appearances, and it is with no difficulty that scholars have identified her as the folk-tale embodiment of the Celtic horse-goddess Epona, in her British form, Rigantona. In fact it is altogether horse-theme country, as one cannot help feeling even now, at Llanybydder Fair or down those lanes where it is normal to find a farmer leading a small, wiry pony, or up on Mynydd Preseli where the wild horses graze, or, as we shall see, on the sheep-grazed slopes of the Brecon Beacons where farmers on horseback gather their flocks, or further south even, where cockle-gatherers ride out in their carts onto the sands. Rigantona is alive and well.

There is a ruined castle on a round knoll at Narberth, with a fine outlook over the wooded rolling countryside of Dyfed, which makes as good a place as any to sit and wait for wonders. But no horsewoman comes riding out of the valley and up past the mound, and possibly this is because, according to some theorists, this is in fact not the true site of Pwyll's mound. The rival castle-mound is an obscure one near Templeton, a few miles south.

Arberth, however, has traditionally been located at Narberth, where the castle, now a fine and evocative ruin, was built by a Norman land-owner in 1246.

The road from Haverfordwest to Carmarthen crosses, at right angles, that from Cardigan to Tenby, a little way to the

north of Narberth. It too passes, at Whitland, ruins which are
of more significance than their appearance would suggest.
The Abbey of Whitland, founded in 1143, was to give rise to
those perhaps more notable monastic foundations of South
and Mid Wales which flourished during the next century. Its
offshoots, which included Strata Florida in Cardiganshire,
were largely responsible for the strong Cistercian movement
which so greatly influenced Welsh religious life up to the end
of the Middle Ages. Moreover tradition says that it was at
Whitland, long before, that Hywel Dda, the Law-giver, had
called the meeting which approved his famous laws, in A.D.
930. There is, unfortunately, no evidence either for the
gathering or for the authorship of the laws, which are only
ascribed to Hywel by later writers. The laws themselves, of
course, were real enough, but their earliest versions are from
the thirteenth century.

The river Taf flows down between Whitland and Carmarthen to join the Tywi, and the two together meet the
Gwendraeth from Kidwelly to form a vast expanse of tidal
water, of tidal mud and sand, spread with seabirds and
cockles, its level stretches throwing into focus the beautiful
hills of its banks. One gets an intimation of the size of it all
when the road comes down to touch the coast at Pendine,
where five miles of hard sand stretch out of sight, inviting
one to find a use for them. Such was once found, and
Pendine Sands now evoke for many those pioneering days
when, in the spirited manner of the 1920s, the world's new
toy, the automobile, was stretched to its limits here. On 25th
September in 1924 Sir Malcolm Campbell averaged 146.16
m.p.h. at Pendine. But most of all we remember, inevitably,
the sad end of J. G. Parry-Thomas, killed by the broken chain
of his car 'Babs', which then, with a romantic gesture worthy
of the place and the endeavour, was buried on the beach. It
lay there not for ever but until a spring day in 1969, when it
was exhumed by an enthusiast who, over the next few years,
painstakingly and expertly restored it.

Laugharne Burrows, sandhills and salt-marsh, flank the
coast where Pendine Sands become the still greater extent of
Laugharne Sands; and the road in this direction runs a little
inland to approach, under Sir John's Hill, Laugharne itself.

The village is pretty, the castle by the water magnificently crumbling. It is an old town, and feels it, plentiful with solid pubs and crouching cottages. Rhys ap Gruffydd, of the house of Dinefwr, built the castle in the twelfth century, while the Normans had not yet fully established themselves in this part of South Wales. The main street, though, stone-built and traditional, tells you little of the real nature of Laugharne, which is that it is on the estuary of the Taf. To get this feeling clearly one has to take that unexpected side road through the quiet, self-effacing cottages, to come out into the lane which tilts down past the Boat House, stuck on that cliff overlooking the streamways and tidal reaches of the zinc mud and silk water. "My seashaken house On a breackneck of rocks ..."

> By scummed, starfish sands
> With their fishwife cross
> Gulls, pipers, cockles and sails,
> Out there, crow black, men
> Tackled with clouds, who keep
> To the sunset nets,
> Geese nearly in heaven, boys
> Stabbing, and herons, and shells
> That speak seven seas ...

Dylan lived in the Boat House during his last years in Wales, and he worked in a shed which he called "the shack" stuck high over the house by the side of the lane from the village. A window of it looks out over the water, so that the words, above, of the Prologue to his *Collected Poems*, must have been an immediate description of what he saw, and what he often saw, while sitting at the small wooden table which was the shed's only furniture. John Malcolm Brinnin describes it as it was:

As a whole, the studio was a rat's-nest of chewed, rolled and discarded papers — piles of manuscripts, unanswered (often unopened) letters, empty cigarette packages, small stacks of literary periodicals, tradesmen's bills, and publishers' brochures. Snatches of reworked poetry lay under empty beer bottles. Volumes of poetry mouldered where they had been placed months, years, before.

Besides its single table and two straight-backed chairs, the studio contained three or four half-filled cartons of books, and a small black coal-burning stove.

Though born in Swansea, the son of a school-master, David Thomas, Dylan had by then come to regard Laugharne as his home. The town already contained one distinguished writer in the form of Richard Hughes, who lived, when Dylan first came there, in a house immediately under the castle. It was Augustus John, on a visit to Hughes in Laugharne, who first introduced Dylan to Caitlin, his future wife, who was modelling for John at the time. The painter also introduced the couple to the Boat House, which, "a stage house with a certain air of mystery about it," he felt would suit them. It seems that Dylan was never very clear about why he came to Laugharne, nor why he stayed.

I've been living now for fifteen years, or centuries, in this timeless, beautiful, barmy (both spellings) town, in this far, forgetful, important place of herons ... pubs, mud, cockles, flatfish, curlews, rain, and human, often all too human, beings.

Some people, he said, live in Laugharne because they were born in Laugharne and saw no good reason to move; others have migrated there for varied reasons.

And some, like myself, just came, one day, for the day, and never left; got off the bus, and forgot to get on again.

There can be little doubt that much of the town's personality contributed to that best-known, word-rich work of his, *Under Milk Wood*. Laugharne, "with its seven public-houses ... one policeman, three rivers, a visiting sea." But the germ of the theme, the mad small town by the sea, had been with him for years. During the war he had spent some time in New Quay, an equivalent but more obviously pretty little harbour town on the Cardiganshire coast. His script about it, *Quite Early One Morning*, was broadcast in 1945. There, in miniature, is the town and population of Llareggub, which, eight years later and with the accumulated richness of Laugharne village life, and with, perhaps a nostalgia and sense of distance learnt from his America experiences, he finally put together, in Laugharne and Boston, in the turmoil of his last few months.

It is not Laugharne, of course, which is described, despite the shop-keepers and the gossip and the pub-haunting cronies, nor is it entirely, specifically, Wales, in spite of the atmosphere of close village life and the sour remarks of the neighbours. The Welshness of the play is export-oriented, a rather stagey caricature. Organ Morgan and Mrs Ogmore-Pritchard are stereotypes, whom one would not seriously expect to find in the twentieth-century flesh. What is actually genuinely Welsh about it is the viewpoint; oblique, allusive, subtly able to insert, by implication rather than in the outright boasts and bombast which are probably all bluff, an underlying basis of unaffected emotion. On this, in the end, all the glib, bawdy, punning, often facile fun is solidly based. Nor is this quality at all imposed: it comes, as if by accident, out of the bits and pieces which run haphazardly together. An overall feeling for something more than a single typical town and its imperfect people emerges. It is a work which is, in the proper sense, romantic. All Welsh writers (and probably painters too), even when anglicized, belong to the romantic tradition.

Much of Dylan's poetry (in spite of his claim that he was seeking clarity) is syntactically and linguistically complex to the point of being, in places, incomprehensible. Some of it becomes really meaningful only when read aloud, and preferably by its author; and such a use of words is perhaps a little outside the demands of the ordinary lover of poetry. There is even room for doubt about whether this verbal complexity is either necessary or desirable. Strings of words can become, as far as communication is concerned, remarkably counter-productive. In fact if it were not for the directness and effectiveness of some of the less pretentious pieces, one would conclude that the thesaurian vocabulary masked, like e e cummings's lack of punctuation or Modigliani's stretched faces, an underlying spirit of banality which, without it, would produce works which were visibly trite. Those who have the patience, and the wish, to sift the bogus from the real, can find in Dylan Thomas's poetry some instances of feeling for which the wording is not unwarranted self-indulgence. For some of course, there is the easy assumption that anything beyond their comprehension must be of deep significance and importance. For many the area threatens a distasteful wallow in verbosity, and for many more the necessary disentangling is simply not worth the effort.

For these reasons, perhaps, *Under Milk Wood* is, ultimately, all that many people really know of Dylan Thomas. It has, on an immediate level, the powerful word-spells and images which one recognizes as poetic. It also has, to a greater extent than many of his works, the porportion-giving element of humour, through which anybody, without practice or qualifications, can approach it. It is probably under the influence of these factors that people usually approach Laugharne; but they will find in this quiet and attractive village hardly a trace of Polly Garter and Captain Cat, and only the faintest shadows of the cobble-streets and the churchyard and the 'Sailors Arms'.

Laugharne is on the Taf, and on its neighbour the Tywi similar waterside villages (though lacking the aura of fame and eccentricity) squat picturesquely between water and hills. Ferryside and Llanstephan face each other distantly across the wide tidal sands. The latter in particular, with its castle on the hill, has an air of peaceful withdrawal, that sort of retirement from the world which estuaries, with their horizontal perspectives and the liquid sounds of their bird-life, seem to generate.

The river fills quickly. Only a few miles north it is narrowed to the size of a stream. It flows, still greatly affected by the tides, through the edges of the town of Carmarthen, a town, in fact, which owes its location partly to the crossing point, there, of a still navigable river. It was the lowest bridging point of the Tywi, and the river at that place can take craft of up to 300 tons.

Although nobody could really call Carmarthen beautiful, it is the sort of place for which one can come to feel a mild affection. Natural, arbitrary, accidental, its fragmented charm

suffering in patches from outbreaks of squalor, it sits
clustered around the coincidence of the A48, A40, and the
river Tywi.

The place has had its ups and downs, and the effect of
degeneration and recovery is visible in its fabric. It is, in spite
of everything, a place of substance, with a population of
about 13,000, and a historic development going back to, at
the very least, A.D. 75. Then, as the Roman field fort
Moridunum, it formed one of the most westerly footholds of
the legions in their invasion of South Wales. Recent excava-
tion has revealed the indications of a civil settlement besides
the fort, and in one way and another it is clear that
Carmarthen was, from an early time, regarded as important.

The name is often said to be derived from 'Caer Myrddin',
the fortress of Myrddin, a dark-age poet and prophet who, in
the hands of Geoffrey of Monmouth, became, through
translation, the Merlin of legend. The story starts elsewhere,
and at its root lies an event of critical importance to British
history.

After the Roman withdrawal, completed about A.D. 410,
there was a period during which the country as a whole
lacked leadership. From about 425 to about 461 a high-king
existed, in the person of Vortigern, who had at least some
pretensions to domination of the whole of Britain. But his
power was inadequate, and he found himself in trouble with
the northern tribes. To the south and east at the same time
the country suffered from raids by ferocious Saxons, and, in
a moment of what must have seemed to him, initially, to be
supreme ingenuity, Vortigern synthesized the two sides of
the problem. He employed the Saxons to fight the rebellious
northerners. "Those wild Saxons," rages Gildas, with the
hindsight of a century's passage and experience of the
unfortunate results, "of accursed name, hated by God and
men." Gildas is categorical in his pinpointing of this mistake.
"Nothing more hurtful, certainly, nothing more bitter,
happened to the island than this."

The result of Vortigern's ploy was, perhaps, even at the
time, predictable. The Saxons lost no time and at once began
complaining "that their monthly supplies were not copiously
contributed to them". They made this the excuse to break

the contract, and at once started to overrun the country. Vortigern was in greater trouble than before.

The ninth-century historian Nenius takes up the sequel. The king called together his wise men, who advised him to retreat to the remote boundaries of his kingdom, and to build there a strong fortress. It sounded like good advice, and Vortigern set off for the area of Snowdon, in North Wales; and the background to this section of the story is given in *Portrait of North Wales*, the companion volume to this book. The citadel he tried to build there, however, made no progress; what was built during the day fell down at night. Again he called his wise men together, and they told him (perhaps implying that it was impossible) to sacrifice on the spot a boy without a father.

Geoffrey of Monmouth, writing in the 1130s, uses this old story as the platform on which to stage the entrance of his hero Merlin, the prophet-wizard whom he had concocted from the Roman-British leader Emrys and the northern poet Myrddin ap Morfryn.

Messengers were immediately sent out through the different parts of the country to find such a person if they could. They came to a town which was afterwards called Kaermerdin and there they saw some lads playing by the town gate. They went to look at the game. Tired by their journey, they sat down in a circle, still hoping to find what they were seeking. At last, when much of the day had passed, a sudden quarrel broke out between two of the lads, whose names were Merlin and Dinabutius. As they argued, Dinabutius said to Merlin: "Why do you try to compete with me, fathead? How can we two be equal in skill? I myself am of royal blood on both sides of my family. As for you, nobody knows who you are, for you never had a father."

On this rather slight evidence the messengers took action; the boy, (whose father, according to his mother's story, had actually been a spirit "in the form of a most handsome young man" which visited her in the convent where she was secluded), was taken to the king, and ultimately saved himself from sacrifice in Snowdonia by displaying his precocious wisdom; and the town of Carmarthen received the name which it still bears. As so often, however, historical accuracy has to spoil a pleasant illusion. The name was probably existent before Merlin's time, and no doubt comes from Moridunum, sometimes spelt Maridunum, the name of the Roman settlement.

The Norman castle (which became the county gaol) was built on the site of an earlier fortress, once a seat of the Princes of South Wales. When Giraldus came through Carmarthen part of the earlier town walls, which he said were made of brick, were still standing. Not much even of the later castle is there now, but it had in its time seen events of some importance. The town was an English stronghold during the early thirteenth century, and was taken by Llewelyn the Great in five days in 1215. In the next rebellion Owen Glendower besieged and took the castle, in 1403. Between these two events Carmarthen had become a borough, receiving its charter in 1313, by which time it was already an important and flourishing town.

In the twelfth-century church is an effigy of the great Rhys ap Thomas, who raised a force to support Henry Tudor on his invasion in 1485. Sir Richard Steele, the dramatist, is also buried there, having fled to this obscure retreat from London largely to avoid his creditors. In the nineteenth century Carmarthen featured briefly in the story of early industrial unrest, when its workhouse was attacked and ransacked during the "Rebecca" riots. And at about the same time it benefited by the extension to Brunel's Great Western Railway, which linked Swansea and Carmarthen to Milford and the boat for Ireland.

Carmarthen's most absurd and, in a way, most appealing ancient monument is its famous oak tree, Merlin's Oak. Tradition says that when it falls, so will Carmarthen; and no effort has been spared to ensure that, technically, it has not yet fallen. There is, however, hardly anything left of it, and what there is (wormeaten and thoroughly dead) is artificially kept from collapse by massive reinforcements of concrete and iron. The analogy is far from accurate. Carmarthen itself is by no means rotten, and no extrinsic aid is needed to keep it in place. It goes on, busy with commerce and agriculture, its streets and shops chattering gently and bilingually with the soft local speech. Maybe there is a universal law to the effect that people are as nice as they sound, and certainly the mouthed vowels and swallowed consonants of the West Glamorgan and Carmarthen area serve to express a friendly and open-hearted attitude. Relaxed, easy-going, the people of the district give the feeling that they are not greatly worried by the world's turbulence and the pressures of the times.

The Tywi runs under the town, thick and cloudy, and at high tide, in the salmon season, the coracle men come down carrying their black boats on their backs. They continue an unchanging trade, the commercial fishing of salmon and sewin (the form of sea-trout common in some Welsh rivers), as a serious profession and by no means to entertain the tourists. The Tywi coracle is slightly blunter and rounder than that used on the Teifi, and the forms are in fact only the two main ones of several possible designs.

North and east the Tywi and the A40 rise towards Llandeilo and the mountains above Llandovery. South the road to Kidwelly and Llanelli follows the line of the river until the two join the Gwendraeth, and the bulk of Cefn Sidan Sands and Towyn Burrows blocks off the normal contact between land and sea.

PART TWO

SWANSEA BAY

V   THE AREA OF SWANSEA

The land is seamed with rivers, draining the broad coastal plateau out into tidal bays. It is the Gwendraeth Fach, no very large river, which flows out at Kidwelly. Coming down quiet country valleys with brown-green salmon pools, it passes below the castle and through the town. The Gwendraeth Fawr meets it from a parallel line to the south, and at a point below the town the estuary suddenly becomes disproportionately large for either river, and they both, among tracts of mud and sand, become for a short time, jointly, the Gwendraeth.

Kidwelly is a small country town, once an important (though never large) centre of the area, now something of a backwater as its enormous neighbours to the south (Burry Port with a monumental power station, Llanelli, where some 4,000 people are engaged in making cars, and Swansea with its major industries spreading down the coast) have expanded far beyond the scope of Kidwelly's medieval conception.

Castle and Church look out at each other across damp river meadows. They are both in fine form, the one rearing bulkily on its slope, the other tall-spired and graceful on the valley bottom.

The first castle at Kidwelly was built early in the twelfth century, following the advance of the Norman lords into the southern part of South Wales. After the death of Henry I (whose reign had been the main period of invasion) there was a short time of confusion, and the Welsh, under the sons of the Lord Rhys, succeeded in re-occupying the area more than once. Kidwelly Castle was then held by the Welsh for many decades, and only finally reverted to Norman possession in the 1240s.

That, of course, is still a very early date for a castle, and in fact most of the impressive battlements confronting us today belong to a slightly later time. The oldest part of the present castle is the inner ward, a curtain wall with four round towers, standing squarely within the arc of the outer wall. This belongs to that great period of castle-building, the late thirteenth century. The chapel tower, which, because of its octagonal appearance, forms such a conspicuous feature of the outside of the castle as seen from the river bank, was added to the inner ward during the next few years. It forms a strangely asymmetrical lump on the side of the castle, and it is perhaps this, more than anything else, which gives Kidwelly its individuality.

The outer curtain, with a splendid southern gatehouse, followed shortly after the construction of the inner ward and chapel tower. Thus Kidwelly was complete by about the year 1330; the plainly later gabled buildings inside were added during the fifteenth century. The castle does not seem to have played a prominent part in history, and apart from its several changes of hands during uprisings and invasions, served mostly as a home for its owner at the time.

The castle, the fourteenth-century church, and a ruined gateway of what was once the town walls, provide, along with the medieval bridge over the Gwendraeth, enough evidence of Kidwelly's age. Modern Wales begins not far away, where Llanelli expresses for Wales today — with images such as Rugby and Industry — what Kidwelly's church and castle do so well for the Middle Ages.

Not that, to first appearances, Llanelli has much to do with this present era. It has its roots firmly in the last century, and miles and miles of terraced housing conspicuously surrounds it. But there is, largely out of sight, much in Llanelli that is brand new. Its courageous approach to the town centre shopping problem, for instance, gives to the place a flourishing and cheerful aspect which less progressive towns have not yet been able to achieve. By contrast, the streets which still have traffic in them seem sad and outdated, a rundown, nobody-cares, feeling about them. The effect of the traffic-free streets is to release that activity which is, perhaps most of all, characteristic of this area. It

Swansea from Town Hill

allows people to stand and chatter.

In Llanelli they chatter largely in Welsh, since the town, unlike Swansea, has not become anglicized as it became modern. It is a Welsh modern town. Everything about it is Welsh, and not least, to an extent in fact to conform to the caricature image of South Wales, the Rugby ground of Stradey Park outside the town, one of the places of pilgrimage for those to whom the sport carries an emotive significance rivalling even that of nationalism.

Hardly out of Llanelli, one is into Swansea, the outskirts of which sprawl now (in contrast to the constricted original city) in all directions, to form a pool of urbanization which sweeps in an arc through Morriston in the north to Port Talbot down the coast of the bay. Quite soon (they say) it will be lapping at the shores of Pontardulais and Pontardawe, still so far separated from it by strips of countryside.

Though probably originally a Scandinavian settlement – some speculate that its name derives from Sweyn, a Nordic leader – Swansea comes into recognizable existence some-where around 1100, when, as a Norman Marcher Lord's fortress and seat, (like so many other old Welsh towns), it formed the administrative centre of the newly-conquered Lordship of Gower. Then for centuries it remained small and obscure, and only with the rise throughout South Wales of the metal-working industry, at the beginning of industrial times, did it start its climb to prominence.

Swansea was the capital of copper. From about 1717 copper smelters existed at Llansamlet and Landore, in its northern outskirts. Some time during the eighteenth century it overtook Neath in this respect, benefiting from better shipping facilities. The harbour was enlarged, for the purpose of this business, in 1791. In 1796 John Morris, of Fforest Copper Works, built a town to house his workers, thus creating Morriston, which has now become merged with the city. The copper ore came from Cornwall, and with it came the chief copper family, the Vivians, the third of whom, after the move to the Swansea area, became the first Lord Swansea, in 1893. By 1860 Swansea was the centre of the copper industry everywhere, completely dominating world trade.

Kidwelly Castle

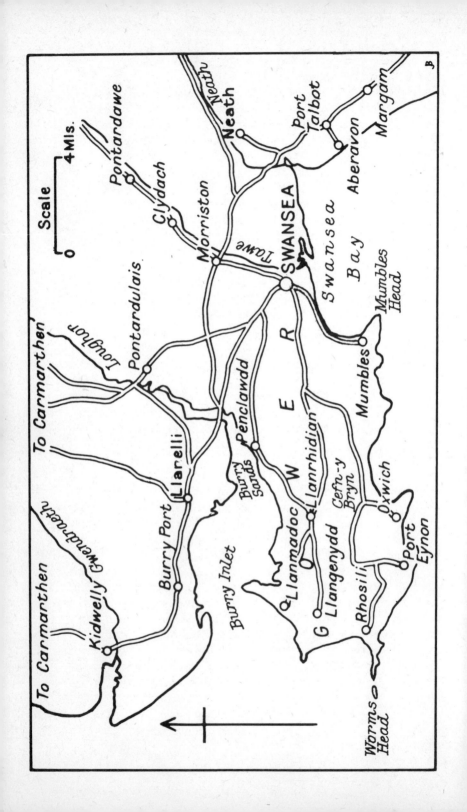

After 1860, however, the native ores on which the smelting business had been built up had started to decline. Swansea continued doggedly by using imported ores, and imports reached a peak during the late 1880s. It was then that the foreign producers of the ores started to build their own smelters.

Several of the by-products of copper-smelting, physically and economically, had in the meantime come to play effective roles. Sulphuric acid was one, and its presence began to involve the Swansea area in the chemical industry. A labour-force skilled in metal-working was another. Both these things, moreover, found a common outlet in the tinplate industry which arose to take the place of copper-smelting.

The rolling of steel plates for tinning was a technique developed at Swansea by William Siemens, who had a factory at Landore during the 1870s. Basically, the sheets were rolled in a pack, split, pickled in sulphuric acid, then tinned by being passed through a bath of molten tin. The industry depended (and depends) of course, on the progress of the steel-making enterprises nearby; and the great iron-works of the northern area converted to steel-making during the '70s and '80s. In Swansea it relied also on the rise of the docks, which had in turn benefited by the increase in coal-exporting. The North and South Docks at Swansea opened in 1859; the Prince of Wales Docks in 1881. (These were later joined by the King's Docks, in 1909, and the Queen's, in 1920). In 1850 the South Wales Railway linked Swansea to Paddington, an event which was celebrated by, among other things, a breakfast to which 690 people sat down.

Tin-plate making rose fast in importance, and had taken over from copper-smelting by 1875. A new outlet for tin was being opened up during the 1850s and '60s, none other than that great canning country, the U.S.A. Even at that period, it seems, Americans liked to have their goods, whenever possible, in cans. Three hundred and twenty-five thousand tons of tin-plate went over the Atlantic in 1891. Swansea and Llanelli — the latter, with seven tinplate works dominating its commercial life, came to be called 'Tinopolis' — benefited for a time from this unpredicted boom. 1891, however, was both the peak and the end of the American expansion. New tarifs led to the loss of the market, and hence to the need to find other outlets.

Swansea had, in the meantime, become a major port, with the result that it was in a position to develop new industries. The many small tinplate works which by then existed continued in production, some of them until the second world war, and the industry is now extant, though rolled largely into one enormous unit, in the form of British Steel's vast Trostre tinplate works at Llwynhendy. This, (part of a policy of siting new sources of employment in the areas which had been losing their old industries), works in conjunction with the steel complex down at Margam, which provides the plate which Trostre then tins.

Though for a time during the early nineteenth century Swansea tentatively tried its hand at being a seaside resort, the city itself has never really been anything but industrial. Mumbles provided the seaside, the yacht-clubs, the beach hotels, the tree-lined promenade. Horse-drawn trams carried people to the sea in 1804, being converted to steam in 1877, and eventually electrified. The Mumbles Railway, said to be the first passenger-carrying railway in the world, unfortunately closed in 1960. With it perhaps went the last vestige of the romantic, pre-war image of Swansea-as-it-was. During the 1950s the separate townships which made up the total identity became increasingly merged and blurred. New works on new sites broke up the old patterns of life, and, as transport improved, the poor communications which had been a barrier to previous integration gave place to the birth of dormitory suburbs and of universal travelling to work. Twenty-five thousand people are employed in the various branches of the steel-works complex, and industrial estates at Llanelli and Pontardawe mop up the hinterland.

The new industries are in fact vast and few. The oil refinery at Llandarcy (which, in 1921, was the first in Britain) has now expanded to an annual throughput of 8 million tons of crude oil. This, together with a major petrochemical plant at the mouth of the Neath river, and also the Margam steel-works, receives its oil direct by pipeline from the Milford Haven terminal.

Communications (which started with the docks and the

railway) have always played a big role in Swansea's history. Now it is to be linked to the Motorway past Cardiff and Newport, and hence both with the English Midlands and with London. Swansea's biggest change, however, was not of this simple economic kind. Most other major cities are, during the 1970s, being systematically destroyed and redeveloped. Forty-one acres of central Swansea, however, had already been destroyed in 1941 by German bombs. There were no old buildings in the city centre left to be blitzed by today's developers.

The reconstruction of the bombed centre took place largely during the 1960s, and to some extent has led to a pleasant and spacious town. The streets are wide, the buildings inoffensive. The physical nature of the place, however, governs its layout. It is on a thin coastal strip, set at the bottom of steep slopes. The terraced houses do their best, climbing the hill precipitously above the city, but are forced eventually to spread down over the back and out of sight. Below, as one sees it from Town Hill, it scarcely has room for grandeur or design. Crammed into its narrow breezy border of the bay, between the limiting factors of the docks on one side and, on the other, wooded Singleton Park, the central area suffers from acute land-shortage. The town itself, therefore, more or less has to take place elsewhere.

Yet this is not entirely sufficient excuse. The main buildings are dotted haphazardly about the place, as if no-one had understood that above all other things a city needs a centre. The Guildhall, which should have been its focus, is stuck out at St Helen's. What must be considered (for lack of rivals) to be its main square, is dominated not by major public buildings but by a not particularly imposing hotel. And over all the town is evenly spread a lack of identity which counterparts (if it is not caused by) this irritating lack of a hub.

Much of Swansea now is respectable and middle-class in attitude, not the robust and salty place of its old images. One catches a faint tang of what it should be, sometimes, in the covered market (largest in Wales) where hordes of cockle-women from the villages of Gower promote their buckets of shells and bags of laverbread with an undiminished, unurban-

ized, enthusiasm. Swansea Market, at its best towards the
weekend, can be a busy and raucous place fully in keeping
with the social traditions which one associates with the city.
When the students are up, also, (and the University, in
Singleton Park, has multiplied its number by three during the
decade from 1960 to '70, bringing its predominantly South
Welsh student body up to 3,500), they inject into the sedate
life of the town a little vitality. But on the whole it is as quiet
and sober as . . . As a wet Sunday afternoon.

It was six o'clock on a winter's evening. Thin, dingy rain spat and
drizzled past the lighted street lamps. The pavements shone long and
yellow. In squeaking goloshes, with mackintosh collars up and
bowlers and trilbies weeping, youngish men from the offices bundled
home against the thistly wind —

Or again:

It was a cold white day in High Street, and nothing to stop the wind
slicing up from the docks, for where the squat and tall shops had
shielded the town from the sea lay their blitzed flat graves marbled
with snow . . .

When Dylan Thomas remembers Swansea, the town of his
childhood, it is cold and wet. Coming back poignantly in
"Return Journey" he finds it moreover flattened and covered
in snow. We do not need to wonder what, as a young man, he
was like, because he several times tells us: "Thick blubber
lips; snub nose; curly mousebrown hair; one front tooth
broken after playing a game called Cats and Dogs, in the
Mermaid, Mumbles; speaks rather fancy . . . lived in the
Uplands."

They lived, actually, in Cwmdonkin Drive, near
Cwmdonkin Park, in the upper, residential part of the town,
in the general area called the Uplands. The houses around the
Park are substantial and respectable, and the Park itself,
where Dylan spent much of his boyhood, is a lovely stretch
of gardens, with, because of its tilted stance on the top of the
town's slope, some fine outlooks to the sky.

Dylan (who was born in 1914) was the son of the English
master at Swansea Grammar School, where he went when he

was eleven. Purists, who quite often get things wrong, persist
in supposing that his name is correctly pronounced, as indeed
the rules of Welsh pronunciation could possibly make it,
'Dullan'. To him, however, it was pronounced as if it were an
English word, and all who actually had dealings with him
accordingly say it as 'Dillan'. Though both his parents were
thoroughly Welsh, he was to a large extent brought up in an
English tradition. To be precise: he did not speak his native
language, a fact for which now, in such different times, his
fellow-countrymen cannot quite forgive him. Possibly it is
this anglicization (for which we may in turn blame Swansea)
which has prevented his ever gaining the status of a national
hero. He is, indeed, more remembered and revered in
Greenwich Village today than in the Uplands.

Those who knew him say, not without tenderness and
regret, that he was a horrid little boy. And the anguish and
turmoil which he brought down on his friends make it seem
likely that he remained, in many ways, a horrid little boy all
his life. His friends found they spent much time and effort
trying to look after him, quite without success.

He left school at seventeen, by which time it was the
1930s and a hard and cold time in South Wales. For a bit he
worked on the Swansea weekly, *Herald of Wales*, but it was
by then inevitable that he should leave, more than a little
embittered, for London.

His first book of poems was published in 1934 (*Eighteen
Poems*), and publications continued during the 1930s. During
the war he worked with the BBC, and, while continuing to
publish verse, started to make those short broadcasts for
which he perhaps became, in his lifetime, best known. The
quality of his voice, fortunately preserved on record, made
whatever he did, humorous or poetic, seem richer and livelier
than printed words, however dextrous, ever could.

During the '40s he returned to Wales, (settling in the Boat
House at Laugharne in 1949), and early in the 1950s made
those three successive and, ultimately, disastrous trips to
America, where he died in November 1953, not long turned
39. *Under Milk Wood*, which in places betrays, perhaps, an
underlying bitterness about Wales, was more or less complete.
His wild, schoolboy life, and the glamour which, for some

reason, is attached to heavy drinking, together with the
legend-making attribute of an early death, have given him a
status which his literary works on their own might never have
achieved. In Wales he is felt to be a slight embarrassment,
being no real part of Welsh culture, and, to the extent that he
dealt with Wales, pressing a little too hard on the national
weak points. In a similar way Kazantzakis is not much loved
in Crete.

A rather feeble memorial in Cwmdonkin Park is all that
there is to see, now, of Swansea's perhaps most famous
citizen. The city's only other claim on the attention of the
outside world is its possession of the Empire Panels which Sir
Frank Brangwyn had intended for the House of Lords.

Swansea is evidently very proud of these; the concert hall
of the Guildhall, where they are housed, is called the
Brangwyn Hall. It is a vast room, the climax of the whole of
the Guildhall's coarsely sumptuous, fascist design. Yet for all
its size and self-conscious magnificence the panels dominate
it completely. To a remarkable degree they both fit and suit
the rooms. The Guildhall's architecture and decor has the
same level and type of nastiness running through it as have
these vast, obsessively intricate expanses of violent colour.

The panels are supposed to represent the races of the
British Empire, and are the product of many years of careful
work. They were to be the memorial to peers who died in the
1914-18 war, but were rejected, in 1930, as being not
suitable for the purpose. Brangwyn was, however, a highly-
respected painter, and Swansea may well have been highly
pleased with its acquisition.

He was born in 1867, in Bruges, though of Welsh parents;
and started his painting career at the age of fifteen as an
apprentice to William Morris. He exhibited at the Royal
Academy as early as 1885, and in 1906 was commissioned to
provide murals for the Royal Exchange. From then on this
became increasingly his line of work. Among other places
where these large and highly-coloured works may be seen are
the Capitol, Missouri, the Court House of Cleveland, Ohio,
the Rockefeller Centre in New York, and the new Parliament
buildings of Winnipeg. He was knighted in 1941, and died
in 1956.

The Brangwyn Panels in Swansea belong to a period of taste patently obsessed with exoticism. They depict strange and profuse creatures and plants in unnatural colours, enmeshed together in a mass of overwhelming vegetation to give an overall effect of claustrophobia; an unnerving excessiveness which, more than anything, suggests madness. Together with the hall itself they present a work of such vast vulgarity that it is hard to understand how anyone, even at the most sombre civic Wagner concert, can keep a straight face.

Though Swansea spreads, and threatens to spread, more than it used to, there is still green countryside around it, as there is on the edge of all South Welsh towns, however big and busy. Development is not dominant in the Swansea Valley, where green slopes of woods and fields rise above the housing. The Swansea Canal runs along the valley bottom, where some 800 acres of waste ground are imminently undergoing reclamation. Clydach (with its enormous nickel works) and Pontardawe are the two main towns of the valley, and urban spread has not yet merged them in the mass of the expanding city.

Most noticeably, perhaps, the unspoilt bracken-covered hills come down to the narrow coastal plain at Port Talbot, where the town of Port Talbot itself is quite overshadowed by the monumental scale of the steelworks. The contrast is complete, between the mild, evenly curving hillsides on the one hand; and the violence of the irregular lines and harsh angles on the other.

The steelworks is visually of such magnificence that it would be highly misleading to imply that it is ugly; for one thing, it tends to do such very spectacular things. Orange or yellow smoke pours out of it on the scale of mid-Atlantic clouds; whole oceans of steam rise from its cooling-towers; a spurt of pure flame beyond the concepts of Prometheus shoots from its sky-scraping chimney. On and on it goes, both in time and space, mile after mile, a staggering complexity of pipes and pinnacles, clad in a mass of ominous vapour, never resting, never relaxing its display. The sun going down behind it darkens a few hours early.

The Bessemer process for making steel was discovered in

1856, and the ironworks at Dowlais converted to it almost at once. The rise in the use of steel, particularly for making railways, during the 1870s, forced the other ironworks at Merthyr and Tredegar to convert during the 1880s. Costs at Merthyr, however, drastically increased, for one reason alone: it was now too far inland. The local iron ores, which contained an amount of phosphorus which, at the time, the process was not able to eliminate, were unsuitable for the making of steel. Foreign ores had to be imported, and the cost of taking them up from the coast was, it became apparent, greater than that of bringing coal for the furnaces down. Dowlais moved to East Moors, alongside Cardiff Docks, in 1891. And in the early 1900s the first steel works opened at Port Talbot.

Port Talbot had, in the meantime, been developing as a port for the furnaces of Cwmavon, the valley immediately inland, where iron was being made at the rate of 4,000 tons a year as early as the 1830s. The harbour at Port Talbot was built in 1837, from which imported ores went up the valley. By 1845 there were seven furnaces at Cwmavon, employing 3,000 men.

The Siemens process of making steel was developed (like tinplate-making) at the Siemens factory at Landore during the 1870s. (The essential difference between the Siemens and the Bessemer process was that the Siemens was an open-hearth process, the result being basically the same). The industry started by Siemens expanded in the Port Talbot district, and it was an offshoot of this which started the Port Talbot Steel Company in 1906.

Tinplate-making was, we have seen, by that time flourishing in the Llanelli and Swansea area, and the relation of that industry to steel production clearly made it desirable for the two to come together. Even so it was not until 1947, in response to the urgent need for modernization of the complete industry, that the several steel-works of the area and the Llanelly Associated Tinplate Companies all merged into one. The Steel Company of Wales, which resulted, started business in the early 1950s.

This large amalgam consisted chiefly of the Port Talbot and Margam works of Guest Keen and Nettlefold and of

Baldwins Limited, which had themselves merged to become Guest Keen and Baldwins in the 1930s. Finally the Steel Company of Wales itself disappeared into the British Steel Corporation, which was formed in 1967.

The mass of steel-works at and near Port Talbot is the largest producer of steel in Britain, with an annual capacity of three million tons. It is fed by a harbour capable of taking ships up to 100,000 tons, through which it imports three and a quarter million tons of ore a year. The furnaces are powered by coke, which is first of all itself made, in 310 coke ovens, at the rate of 30,000 tons a week. Figures worthy to counterpart its billowing smoke pour from Port Talbot.

The long series of works takes the process all the way from ore to sheet steel, through crushing plants and blast furnaces and strip mills and coil mills and temper mills. The hot rolled coil goes then to the Corporation's tinplate works, and the cold reduced sheet steel departs to the makers of cars and washing-machines.

Almost as complete in its contrast as the soft lines of the hills on one side of the steel-works belt, is the sandy pleasure-land of Aberavon on its other side. Here another booming industry arises out of the same economic state which gives us that demand for sheets for cars and washing-machines. The leisure business is now, once again, big stuff.

Evidently, to judge from the ambitious scope of Afon Lido and the Entertainment Centre, there is confidence in the future. The same spirit as that which in one century gave rise to Bath and Brighton, and in another to Blackpool and Llandudno, lies behind the recent grandiose construction of Aberavon. But though we may be building new resorts today, the emphasis is now (just as is that of mass production) firmly on the element of quantity. Aberavon's funfair is immense, its swimming-pool of full Olympic size with room for 1,000 spectators, its car-park covers many, many acres, and its crowds come by the tens of thousands. What it lacks, however, is style. The acres of standard housing simply tail off into promenade, along which the new buildings are set down blankly, with a kind of unimaginative optimism. The huge and sparkling beach onto which they face provides a justification for something with much more sense of grandeur.

VI   GOWER

'Gower', one says, or one risks correction. Not 'the Gower', but either 'Gower' or 'the Gower peninsula'. Possibly it is technically correct to maintain that these two do not in fact refer to the same thing. Gower was originally a Welsh territory, the cantref of Gwyr, which later became a Norman lordship. At both periods it included very much more than the narrow, nineteen-mile long peninsula to which the name now usually applies. Swansea was its capital, and it extended northwards up the Swansea Valley. But although the mainland part of this district is sometimes, though more rarely now, known as 'East Gower', the name, whether rightly or wrongly, is now almost always used to mean the small and clearly-defined peninsula itself.

It is not an easy place to get to know. There is an inaccessibility about it which is accurately represented in physical form by the winding lanes and footpaths which lead almost discouragingly to its best features. Much of it you can only get to with difficulty, and one result is that in spite of its really quite small size it evades the fate of being instantly seen and known.

Gower is not, by tradition or population, entirely Welsh, most of it having been Normanized quite early in the twelfth century. The four great castles of Penard, Oystermouth, Weobly and Penrice, erected in the late thirteenth century, show clearly what a grip the invaders had by then established on this small area. But this invasion was of course far from being the first, and these remains, though the most conspicuous, are not, by other standards, really old or greatly ingenious. The mild-weathered, sea-surrounded stretch of inhabitable land was always lived in — since those improbable days, indeed, when the mammoth and the woolly rhino shared the icy countryside with a human species to which we can hardly feel much close relationship.

Gower has Old Red Sandstone summits, but a Carboniferous Limestone coast, and in the cliff caves which so
frequently form in limestone the people of the Old Stone
Age lived, sometime (estimates vary) perhaps rather more
than 20,000 years ago. The bones of one of them was found
at Paviland Cave in 1822, together with the bones of
reindeer, bison, wolf, woolly rhinoceros and mammoth. The
skeleton and the mode of burial are important, since they
show close resemblances with the continental Cromagnon
type, one of the earliest of all forms of *homo sapiens.*

Cromagnon and his descendants of succeeding centuries
were hunters. Only a long time later, in fact, agriculture,
through invading tribes, spread into Britain. With it came,
during the second millennium B.C., the building of those
great stone tombs with which Gower, like most South Wales
coastal regions, is liberally dotted. The Iron Age in turn
brought to this coast, as to others, the builders of ring-forts
and promontory forts, during the last few centuries B.C., and
with these, probably, came the Celtic language.

Swansea is bounded to the south by the headland known
as The Mumbles, a name which now applies to the whole of
the bay-side suburb of Swansea, a long, yacht-crowded
stretch of waterfront which ends with Mumbles Head. Here
two small islands, one of which accommodates a lighthouse
built in the last decade of the eighteenth century, mark the
end of the headland and the boundary of the bay. Mumbles
Pier (where holiday cruise steamers come and go) and the
lifeboat slipway, form further well-known features of the
view, which is in general pleasantly nautical and relaxing.
Though Mumbles doubles as a dormitory for Swansea and as
a small and popular resort, it has a refreshingly natural and
enjoyable atmosphere. Busy with yachting, softened by its
waterfront trees, favoured with splendid views over Swansea
Bay.

Strictly the resort, and village, which it is now so easy to
think of generally as 'Mumbles', is really Oystermouth, and is
of old and respectable standing. Oysters were perhaps fished
from there in Roman times, and certainly the industry
reached a peak during the seventeenth century. In 1684 it
was said that these were the best oysters in Britain. Business

flourished into the 1920s, but came to an end when the oysters were made unpalatable by a disease in 1926. Though the beds are probably still there, and may by now be eatable again, no-one, surprisingly, has so far taken the inititative to rediscover them.

Some slight impressions of this fishing village which preceded the resort can be had in the back streets which climb the hill behind, at the top of which the castle overlooks the whole. This, second in importance in its time to Swansea, was one of the seats of the Lords of Gower. Though there had been a castle here at the beginning of the twelfth century, the present solid keep arose during the middle thirteenth, and the buildings spreading out from it belong to the end of that century and the early part of the next. The chapel tower which juts from the keep was added in the early fourteenth century by the de Mowbray family, then its occupants.

Oystermouth church, which has some fine architectural items, struggling as in so many Gower churches, to overcome the deadening effect of nineteenth century restorations and additions, is notable perhaps most for being the burial place of Dr Bowdler, the physician turned man-of-letters who produced, in 1818, his edition of Shakespeare which has made his name one of the few personal names to enter the language. The bowdlerized ten volumes of the Family Shakespeare, "in which nothing is added to the original text; but those words and expressions are omitted which cannot with propriety be read aloud in a family", was an outstanding successs, and the good man went on to perform the same mutilation to Gibbon's *Decline and Fall*, "for the use of Families and Young Persons". He retired to the Swansea area, and died in 1825.

Over Mumbles Head, then, Gower, as one normally thinks of it, really begins. Those who have known it all their lives complain of it being crowded and commercialized now, but in comparison to other places the nearest it really comes to being popular and crowded is at these next two bays, Langland and Caswell, which are, unlike most pieces of the coastline, quite easily accessible by road. Their proximity to Swansea also ensures that they will not be neglected, and to some extent they serve the valuable function of acting as a filter which prevents too much of the flood from flowing on into the depths of Gower.

A great limestone mass then rears out of the coastline, blocking the way, and the road is forced inland, in a confusion of lanes and junctions around Bishopston. Pwll-du Head is a 300-foot headland over the water, which, like most of the neighbouring stretch of sandy and craggy countryside, is hard to get near to in a car. This area possesses, to the west of Pwll-du, one of the famous bone-caves, Bacon Hole, where traces of a long period of occupation were discovered. Not only bones of elephant, bear and wolf were found, but human artefacts of the Iron Age and Roman period. This is the only one of the caves which is relatively easy to get to; but now there is nothing there to see. The bits and pieces are all in Swansea Museum. Near it again, but slightly less easily accessible, is the larger cliff-face cave called Minchin Hole. It lies a little way along the coast from Fox Hole Bay, which in turn can be reached by the road which runs down to Southgate. Here also were the same collection of exotic bones, together with Early Iron Age pottery and some signs of occupation possibly during early Christian times.

Bishopston is a large and active village now, busy supplying considerable quantities of vegetables to Swansea. These include the traditional, and still greatly popular, edible seaweed, which is continually available in enormous quantities in Swansea Market. Called laver, from the Latin word for a type of water-plant, it is normally, perhaps because mixed with flour or oatmeal, known as 'laverbread'.

The gathering of this harvest is, possibly intentionally, surrounded with a certain mystery. The end result, however, is delicious. The seaweed (a red variety known as Porphyra) is boiled at an early stage, and reaches the market looking like black spinach purée. It is then mixed with a small amount of oatmeal, and sold in half-pound packets. The normal way of cooking it is to cover it with flour or oatmeal and fry it in small cakes in bacon fat. It tastes not, as one would expect, like spinach (though the texture of the taste is similar), nor like anything recognizably to do with the sea. The taste, which is of the order of a meat taste rather than a vegetable, is like none other and therefore can only be experienced, not described.

Much interesting country spreads about from Bishopston and the neighbouring village of Parkmill, and clearly illustrates the point that it is in its complicated wooded interior that the real character of Gower lies. The scenery of the coastline, however striking it may be in parts, does not compare as a whole with those spectacular sweeps of Pembrokeshire, and consequently, for many people, is disappointing. In Gower, however, the country and coast occasionally interact, quiet and wooded valleys running down to deserted beaches, tidal streams winding inland into the groves.

The site of Penard Castle combines these qualities, the ruin impressively overlooking a small-scale, complex valley. The castle is set in the middle of natural country, bounded on one side by a golf course. It is best arrived at from the direction of Parkmill, down the valley of the Penard Pill, by which route the unfolding of the valley and the sight of the castle has its best effect. The castle can in fact be seen from very few places, and can only be approached on foot and by a short walk.

As one comes out of the little wooded valley the view of the castle appears with a dramatic suddenness, up on a crag overlooking the sandy, lovely, empty valley. The small tidal river wanders out onto a normally lonely beach, in its atmosphere removed by centuries from most of modern life, secure as it is in its seclusion from the car-bound public. In Gower, thank goodness, to get to the really worthwhile places one has to walk. The result is that when one gets to them there is usually no-one there.

Penard Castle is a thirteenth-century Norman castle, like so many others, though its romantic perch on the hill makes it feel much older. Little besides that is known about it, and it does not seem to have been of any great importance. The best preserved part of it is, fortunately, that which faces the best viewpoint; on the other side it is crumbling and largely gone. It had fallen into a condition described as "desolate and ruinous" by 1650, and now much of the interior has filled up with sand.

Penard Castle, Gower

There are not many really striking pieces of scenery in Gower, but perhaps that which flanks the estuary of the Penard Pill is one. Three Cliffs Bay, with its prominent, eponymous seascape, can best be seen from the facing slope, where a footpath comes down to overlook the sands from the road which, after leaving Parkmill, comes back at this point towards the sea.

Oxwich Bay, past the next headland, sweeps round in a three-mile curve to terminate in Oxwich village itself, which, though small and undistinguished, is one of the few really seaside villages on this south coast of Gower. The bay is sheltered by the high, empty promontory of Oxwich Point, and enclosed at its back by Oxwich Burrows, sand dunes and salt marshes, which, as a Nature Reserve, provide a good selection of unusual species of birds and plants. The ancient church, founded at Oxwich in the sixth century and in its remaining form of the eleventh to fourteenth, contains a font which is said to have been put there by St Illtyd himself, the founder, to whom so many churches in this part of South Wales are dedicated.

Illtyd (or, equally frequently, 'Illtud') was a highly influential religious leader of the early sixth century. Probably of continental origin, he was born perhaps during the 460s, and came to Britain after a period of studying in Paris. He moved to Glamorgan, at first as a courtier of the regional king, and soon after (following an encounter with a hermit) became a monk and, for a time, a recluse. He founded a monastery at the place which, called after him Llan Illtud Vawr, has over the centuries become contracted to Llantwit Major. The settlement there was agricultural as well as scholarly, and Illtud is credited with the invention of a new way of ploughing which gave greater yields of wheat.

Up above Oxwich much of the area is taken up with Penrice Park, although the small village of Penrice, hidden down narrow lanes, sits, quietly retaining its oldness of character, in between the Park and the coast. This unobtrusive place, traditionally the focus of Gower community life, was once the peninsula's main market town, It is, however, overshadowed by the importance of the nearby castle.

Penrice Castle was the main seat, for some centuries, of the

Worm's Head from Llangenydd beach, across Rhosili Bay

Mansel family, the rich and powerful ruling family of Gower. The old castle was eventually replaced, as the family home, by the mainly Georgian house which today, still occupied, stands in the vicinity of its predecessor. The Norman castle is the largest of the Gower castles; built during the thirteenth century, it consists mainly of an old round keep with an added curtain wall and gatehouse. Perhaps the best known member of the family was Sir Rice Mansel, who rose to a position of power in the time of Henry VIII. The family increased their possessions as a result, and after Sir Rice's time their main residence became at Margam Abbey, near Port Talbot.

Just as the modern Penrice Castle was a contemporary equivalent, as family seat, of this fortress, so not even the thirteenth-century keep and wall were completely unprecedented. A still earlier generation of castle remains near the village, in the form of a huge, overgrown oval embankment, known locally as the Mounty Bank. This was the basis of the first early Norman castle, a timber fortress of raised palisades, which must have been constructed in the years immediately following the Conquest.

The road returns to the coast again at Port Eynon, again one of the few villages of Gower actually on the sea, and there, and at Horton nearby, are plentiful sand-dunes and sandy beaches. The village, once an oyster-fishing port, did a good trade during the nineteenth century in local limestone, which was shipped across the Bristol Channel to Devon, where limestone is a scarce commodity. The marble lifeboat-man whom one can hardly miss in Port Eynon's small, almost cosy streets, is a memorial commemorating a lifeboat disaster in 1916.

Paviland Cave, most famous of all the bone-caves of Gower, is on the long stretch of rather rugged coastline west of Port Eynon. But it is difficult to get to, hard to enter, and there is nothing in it to see once one is there. The bones of the Cromagnon man are in the Oxford University Museum.

Visually the most striking part of Gower is no doubt its far western end, where the combination of Rhosili Bay and Worms Head forms a great set-piece of coastal scenery. The village of Rhosili itself hardly exists, though the church has a fine Norman doorway. The place is famous chiefly for its beach.

Rhosili Bay stretches in a single three-mile sweep of even coastline, bordered with fine sand. The slight curve of its arc, the regular width of the beach, the unbroken line of it, the way it spreads below one, unspoilt, as one comes steeply down from Rhosili, ensure that it is almost unrivalled among beaches. At the back the open grassland of Rhosili Downs insulate it from any habitation; and it is overlooked by Rhosili Hill, the Beacon of which, at 632 feet, is the highest spot in Gower.

The other thing for which Rhosili is rightly famous is the view of Worms Head, a tidal island off the end of the headland, which is Gower's most spectacular and best-known piece of landscape. It is called this (to us) strange name, because of its resemblance to a dragon — 'worm', or 'wurm', being the Old English word for dragon. This thin and long extension to the land is in any case quite snake-like. Visually it provides a perfect counterpart to the long flat expanse of the beach.

The far end of Gower is all natural farming country, quite untouched by modern development. Dunes separate the sea from the villages, where, in the north-western corner, Llangenydd and Llanmadoc sit at the end of small lanes, each with their old church. Of these Llangenydd has the largest, Llanmadoc the smallest, in Gower, the first containing a Celtic gravestone-cover (possibly even that of St Cenydd, the founder) and the second a Celtic cross, and an early tombstone which is now set in its window-sill.

Such villages have, though they are certainly not seaside, the feel, perhaps the smell, of the sea. But it is inland Gower that is strongest in atmosphere — the wooded, lane-threaded centre, with its small-scale, enclosing, intricate scenery. Typical of this intensely rural countryside is, to the east of the mass of Cefn Bryn, the quiet little valley-village of Ilston. The old church (St Illtyd's again) has, like so many in Gower, been badly spoilt by restoration, but the exterior remains impressive. The sturdy battlemented tower has an air of durability which could never be affected by any amount of renovation.

Up a quiet, damp valley near to Ilston one can find the remains, marked with a plaque, of what is said to be the first of Wales's Baptist Chapels. This courageous venture, of 1649–1660, was diplomatically placed thoroughly out of sight, and, like many of the interesting spots of Gower, still remains so. A small winding valley with enclosing trees leads up to it, like many such stream-valleys of the peninsula, and gives to the spot, even in high summer, an inescapably autumnal feeling.

Another green winding, wooded valley in this area is the two-mile long stretch of peaceful country known as Green Cwm. This contains the large chamber tomb and stone mound called Giant's Grave, which, when it was opened in 1869, was found to contain a great number of human burials. Unfortunately the tomb has been meticulously restored by the Ministry of Works, and now looks neat and tidy and completely lacking in antiquity.

In contrast to the general woodedness of central Gower, the bare upland mass of Cefn Bryn gives an outlook and an airy, sky-surrounded feeling not otherwise obtainable on the peninsula. Ponies and bracken, heather and larks, and, when the air is clear of its frequent haze, a view of the other coastlines with which Gower is distantly surrounded. Pembrokeshire sticks out to the west, and thirty miles away to the south is the north Devon coast.

Cefn Bryn is made of Old Red Sandstone, an outcrop of which runs down the middle of the peninsula. It reaches just over 600 feet, a little lower than Rhosili Hill, but by its central position ranks as the most prominent point of Gower. At one of its highest and most outstanding points is the Neolithic chamber tomb called Arthur's Stone.

Cromlechs come in many shapes and sizes, some modest, some, like Pentre Ifan on its Pembrokeshire slope, positively flamboyant. Arthur's Stone, at one extreme, is so enormous as to be absurd. The vast lump of its capstone completely dwarfs the uprights on which it is set. It is, in fact, quite unnecessarily big, so that it is clear that the means (provision of a permanent covering of a communal grave) has become an end in itself (the raising of as large a piece of rock as possible onto the ends of upright stones). The effect presumably

intended was amazement at the skill of this achievement, and
to that extent it works; but there is a side-effect which
cannot have been a part of the original intention. The sight of
this monstrous mass overwhelming the cromlech provokes
something approaching hilarity. There is a quite ridiculous
manner about it, as there is, inevitably, about things which
ultimately amount to showing off. Certainly, however, it
makes its point. One can do anything if one really wants to.

The capstone – said, at what must surely be a modest
estimate, to weigh at least 25 tons – is in fact split in two.
Once it was, incredibly, even larger. The broken piece lies
alongside, itself so big that one would hardly think it possible
to move it. Whether because of a shift in position, or through
miscalculation, the remaining capstone does not rest on all
the uprights, some of which are therefore dispensible. What is
bewildering, (as with the long journey of the Stonehenge
bluestones), about this undoubtedly impressive achievement,
is what motivation can have been so compulsive, in 2,500
B.C., that it drove people to overcome the great difficulties
involved. You would not build Arthur's Stone unless, in some
way or another, you had to.

Salt marshes begin to take over from sand dunes on the
north coast, as one moves east. Llanrhidian village, though
once again not quite on the coast, is a marsh-side place which
once was a weaving centre. Not far away is Weobley Castle,
one of the main Norman castles of Gower, which, unusually,
has been occupied until recent times. The square keep
probably dates from the mid-thirteenth century, the remaining buildings being added during the later part of that
century and the beginning of the next.

This north-east part of Gower is traditionally the Welsh
area, the natives having been consigned by the Normans to
the northern side of 'Welsh Moor'. Its main town is
Penclawdd, which, pre-eminently, is the centre of the
cockle-gathering business.

The cockles grow in beds on the hard sand of the estuary,
on that expanse in front of Penclawdd where the water (a
combination of several rivers), known as the Burry Estuary, is
absent over the distant mud for long periods of the day. They
are gathered by rakes and sieved; fairly strict regulations

govern the permitted size. Every day the inhabitants of Penclawdd go down onto the beach with their ponies and carts, coming back with sacks of cockles, an ancient peasant pastime which persists unchanging into the post-industrial age. Traditionally it is the job of the town's women, while the men are employed in the previously mining villages of Gowerton and Dunvant. Now, in spite of the tinworks and other industries of East Gower, men too are active in the cockle-business. It is hard to appreciate, primitive as it seems, what big money this simple gathering activity can bring. Estimates of the 1950s put the annual turnover from cockles in the Burry Estuary at a quarter of a million pounds. Some sixty tons of cockles passed through Penclawdd every week.

Beyond Penclawdd reality, normality, returns. Wherever Gower formally stops, its ethos of the unmarked, rural past is confined to the peninsula. Gowerton is distinctly urban and industrial, and through it one arrives, imperceptibly, back in the unremarkable outskirts of Swansea.

PART THREE

BRECON BEACONS

VII   BLACK MOUNTAIN AND FFOREST FAWR

A great deal of Wales, but not quite all, is taken up by mountain and coastline. What is remarkable, consequently, is the richness and extent of its river valleys. Approaching the central interior of South Wales through Mid-Wales's complex countryside one gets a good view of this aspect of the country's nature. And any route southwards is inevitably enmeshed with rivers.

Builth Wells, a quiet and grey town with a new function of tourism growing out of its old character of spa and respectable retreat, forms the point of entry into this inland block of South Wales. The town, though solid and stone-constructed, is much less pretentious than its neighbour, Llandrindod Wells. But unlike that grander watering-place, it is lucky enough to be on the incomparable Wye. The river runs at its side, green, soft and slow, and as it passes it enables Builth to parade its advantage, briefly, through the forms of a spacious riverside car-park and a fine old bridge.

A small road runs directly south from Builth Wells, heading for Brecon over Mynydd Epynt. This large, and largely empty, mass of sheep-grazed heathlands, rising to over 1,500 feet, is crossed by only one other road, the ancient drover's track up from the valley near Llanwrtyd Wells. The two roads meet at Upper Chapel, and begin a joint descent down the valley of the Honddu. Up on the heathlands there is that lark-ringing brightness of fresh-air and uncluttered vision characteristic of these domed uplands, where nothing is sharp or linear, all surfaces curving downwards gently under a placid sky.

Horses abound in South Wales. It is a theme, as we have seen, which trots through the whole country. On the lower

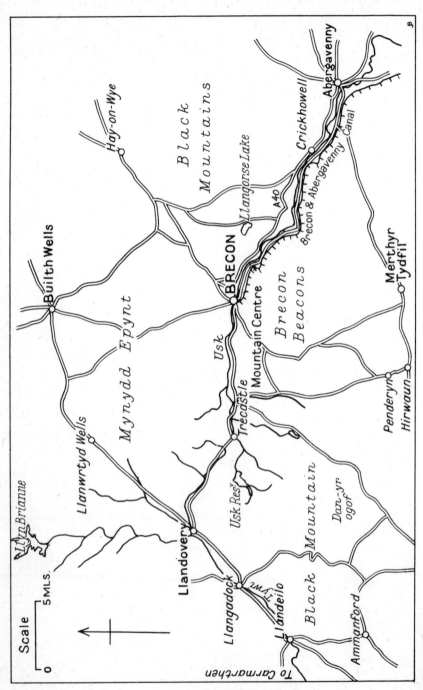

Brecon Beacons

slopes of Mynydd Epynt horses and foals compete with the Welsh Black cattle in those thick-hedged, absurdly green fields. This is, as many people have remarked, a very brightly-coloured county. From Upper Chapel southwards, until the limestone outcrops replace this brilliance with their milder tones in the area of Penderyn and Ystradgynlais, the slopes are liable to be patched with squares of a startling pink or red. Bright red arable fields combine in this patchwork with bright green meadows. It is, in fact, thoroughly sandstone country. The Old Red Sandstone has eroded away to form a new red soil. A great deal about the area of Brecon is explained by reference to this one element: sandstone.

Surprisingly, perhaps, the beautiful area of Mynydd Epynt is not included in the Brecon Beacons National Park. Certainly the drawing of this largely arbitrary line (inside which is a National Park, and outside only ordinary mortal countryside) is a most unenviable job. The Park actually begins just north of Brecon and a large part of it forms, in fact, the view that one gets from the southward slopes of Mynydd Epynt, where the whole of the mountain area is spread out peak by peak. The escarpmented easterly edges of the Beacons themselves give the view a fine, prominent outline.

From Builth Wells two other roads in fact run south, by which, as alternatives, Brecon can be approached. One runs directly and without any great interest down the Wye valley to the east of Mynydd Epynt. The other passes through the pleasant area of Llanwrtyd Wells (itself a much smaller version of the once-fashionable spas) to join the A40 at Llandovery.

Llandovery is not only on the A40 but, like indeed so many substantial valley towns, on a thick brown fishing-river. In fact, in this case, it is on two, the Tywi and the Bran, and takes its name from this circumstance: Llan-ym-ddyfri, church among the waters. It has a market and a public school, and that positive air of being an old-established country town, with the unshakable solidity which is the quality of a prosperous agricultural centre. Sitting squatly in the catchment area of the upper Tywi, it takes in its stride the swarming tourists and the visiting fishermen.

A little north of Llandovery lies one of Wales's newest tourist attractions. Some eight miles up the upper Tywi valley, where dense riparial groves cluster below smooth bracken slopes, one comes, by country lanes, to the giant modern engineering achievement of Llyn Brianne.

The Brianne reservoir differs in several important respects from other, and more notorious, water-undertakings in Wales. Firstly it was not intended, by the planners, that it should be where it is. A reservoir had been planned in an inhabited area a good way further south, in the Gwendraeth valley, nearer to the point of demand. It was largely as a result of public action that that plan was abandoned, and this more remote, and less destructive, site was chosen. A fact which alone would give Brianne a pre-judged value. Unlike some drowned valleys, moreover, that of the Brianne contained no communities, and nothing that one could honestly call valuable agricultural land. But most crucial is of course the question of the water's destination. Tryweryn and Vyrnwy go to quench the endless thirst of the English north-west midlands. But the water from Llyn Brianne flows only into Wales.

It is not entirely, of course, a question of cottage taps. Brianne is there to supply the urban complex of Swansea, in which the largest consumer of water is the steel industry of the Margam and Port Talbot area. It requires no less than 200 tons of water to make one ton of steel; a quantity which is quite intimidating, in view of plans now in progress to raise Wales's steel-producing capacity to ten million metric-tons a year. The effect of this would be to create a further 1,300 jobs, in an area where already 25,000 people are employed in the various steel-works. In this way the demand for water is intricately involved with the overall economic health of the country.

Brianne works, like other modern reservoirs, not as a source for pipelined water, but as a river regulator. Water can be released into the Tywi, which carries it conveniently towards its destination. At Natngaredig, east of Carmarthen, it can then be extracted again, at the rate of 85 million gallons a day, and fed by way of sixty-inch pipes to West Glamorgan. The intention is to work this system together with a similar regulation of the Usk, by means of the Usk reservoir south-east of Llandovery, and the Cray reservoir in the area known as Fforest Fawr, source of a further headstream of the Usk on this northern side of the watershed. Demand throughout South Wales can then, it is envisaged, be adequately met until about 2010.

The reservoir at Brianne cost £21 million to construct, and was opened in the spring of 1973. It consists of two deep gorges, blocked below their junction by the highest dam in Britain. The capacity thus created is some ten thousand million gallons. It is not at all unpleasant to view, a mild and unobtrusive stretch of water in a deep two-armed valley, terminated by some simple and impressive works in modern concrete and unobjectionable grass.

The A40 continues to Llandeilo, down the Tywi, though at Llangadog one may leave it to take the road up into the wilderness of the Black Mountain area. Llandeilo itself would be a pleasant, river-based small town, if it were not for the constant pressure on it of the main road's traffic. The presence of streaming cars in its shopping-street gives to it a crowded, hurried atmosphere which it would otherwise quite lack. Nearby, above the river, is Dinefwr Castle in its extensive private park, the seat of old South-Welsh princes, and of the Lord Rhys who ruled Deheubarth, the kingdom to which he was the heir, with truly feudal independence, in the reign of Henry II. His descendants remained at Dinefwr, (and indeed the Dinefwr family is still there), and it was the seat of that other notable leader, Sir Rhys ap Thomas, who crucially lent his support to Henry Tudor when he launched his attack on the Yorkist monarchy.

A little to the south-east of Llandeilo, just beyond the village of Trapp, lies another impressive castle. Carreg Cennen springs from the edge of a limestone cliff, its towers and walls themselves having the same block-formed nature as the ground they grow from, the same crumbled, jagged line. The castle is in fact a product and extension of the crag's face, being built of the same stone, and placed there specifically to put to use the effects of the natural feature. A fine view of the whole country around, and particularly of the small Cennen valley far below, distinguishes a site which no castle-builder could have brought himself to leave neglected.

It is not known, however, at what date the first fortress on this outcrop came to be constructed. Archaeological finds indicate a Roman occupation of the hill, but almost certainly it would have served tribal and minor dynastic needs even before then. The craggy castle there today, with its familiar features of medieval defensive architecture – the sturdy gatehouse, and the separated wards – belongs to the period of the late thirteenth and early fourteenth centuries. Its first historical mention is in 1248, when one of the descendants of Rhys ap Gruffydd, the prince of Deheubarth to whom Henry II allowed the title of the Lord Rhys, won the castle back from an English family into whose hands it had fallen. It became English property again in 1277, during the invasion of Edward I. The actual building of the castle, in the meantime, is something of a mystery; no records survive, but it is supposed that it was started sometime during the late twelfth century under the auspices of the Lord Rhys of Dinefwr.

It is known that Edward, during his consolidation of power in Wales, granted the castle in 1283 to a Gloucestershire supporter, John Giffard. And it is probably during Giffard's occupation that the present structure, with its characteristically Edwardian features, came into existence. The Giffard family continued in ownership until the 1320s. For the next few decades Carreg Cennen continued to change hands, while various repairs and additions to the structure were made. For a period it came into the ownership of John of Gaunt, whose works on the castle in 1369 are well recorded. Henry IV, being John of Gaunt's heir, was in possession of it when he acquired the throne; and not surprisingly it became a Lancastrian stronghold during the Wars of the Roses. When Edward IV came to power he set about asserting control over South Wales, and one result was the virtual demolition of Carreg Cennen castle. It was rendered no longer usable, and has been little but a striking part of the scenery ever since.

The castle is most impressive at a distance, and particularly seen from the south, out of the Cennen valley itself; unfortunately many of the finest views of it from the road are curtained from the visitor by those high, thick hedges, and one has to stop and climb the bank to peer out over the foliage at the splendidly romantic ruin. Inside, the walls and stairways now seem rather lifeless, preserved as a record of something from which the meaning has quite ebbed away. It has two features, perhaps, which, like its outward appearance, arise directly from the nature of the site. They are both related to the characteristics of limestone.

The first, to the left as one enters, is a lime-kiln, still quite clearly identifiable and in good repair, which was used during the construction of the castle to make, from the limestone outcrops nearby, the mortar which binds the masonry. And there alongside it is the miniature quarry — a rectangular ditch in the slope — from which the raw material was drawn.

The other feature which adds to the castle's individuality is a cave in the rock under the outer ward. Reached by a long sloping tunnel, lit by slits in its outside wall, and itself deep and dark, with the quiet dripping of water in its depths and the one narrow entrance, it has about it a primeval magnetism, something familiar and disturbing. Perhaps a race-memory of home, the first damp dwelling-place of the species; or perhaps, on a different level, an echo of those cramped but safe conditions of the womb.

Although much of the area of the Brecon Beacons National Park is characterized by its formation out of Old Red Sandstone, a long and narrow limestone strip runs along its southern border and touches the northern edges of the coalfield. The geological belts are largely in this east-to-west alignment, so that, crossing them from north to south, one moves quite clearly through their various territories. The road which crosses the area known as the Black Mountain well illustrates the change; coming down towards Brynamman it runs past limestone quarries. This high and scenic road, dropping from more than one-and-a-half thousand feet towards the upper valleys of Ammanford and Ystradgynlais, also gives one a clear feeling of the relation of the coal-based industry to the countryside in which it is largely located.

Places like Brynamman and Cwmllynfell fall between the two worlds, being both on the southern rim of the National Park and on the northern rim of the coalfield. Their position on the edge of the mountain guarantees that they will be airy and light, with fresh winds coming down off the shale and grass slopes. Coal-town architecture (those long rows of neat cottages) juts occasionally into the view of sheep grazing among the limestone boulders. The humped banks of tips loom on the southern horizon. Cows and sheep tend to wander into the streets, and the people dress in country clothes.

Further down, into the anthracite country, the town of Ammanford itself to a great extent typifies the valley towns on the edges of urban South Wales. Being in a hollow surrounded by slopes formed of green fields and copses, it has a constant view of country, giving it the atmosphere of a country town. The anthracite coal is deep under these rolling hills, and, although occasional open-cast mines occur, it hardly affects the scenery at all. You could quite easily not notice that it was there in the area surrounding Ammanford. The land is rich and pleasant and agricultural.

Clearly what is different about the southern belt of the National Park is its colour. To a large extent the underlying character of a place is manifested by the colour of its dust: the grit beside the road, along the footpaths, and on patches of waste ground. It forms the overall impression which you get before you stop to analyse the geological and social make-up. The bulk of the Brecon area is red, giving a strong and clear visual impact; the lower valleys have the mild, neutral tones of their grey stone; once one is in the coal-belt the dust is darker, and black grit fills the hollows of the roadside grass, often unfairly ringing up the label 'sordid' in one's mind.

Eastwards of the road down to Brynamman lies the Black Mountain proper, with its two high points of Carmarthen Fan, reaching 2,460 feet, and the counterparting Brecon Fan which is some two hundred feet higher. Either side of these two tilted, escarpmented ridges lie two small lakes, Llyn-y-Fan Fach and Llyn-y-Fan Fawr. It is the former, eastern of these two, perhaps the less accessible and most enclosed at the foot of the circling crest of the long scarp, which is the better known. It is the extraordinary rock formation, the stratified faces of the high and sheer cliffs, which initially set the strange mood of the place. It lies, moreover, in a wild and unusual area, and has attracted to itself the aura of magic.

A shepherd, a Myddfai man (chants the tale) passing the lake in the evening, saw in this lonely place a beautiful woman emerging from the water. He fell in love with her, and when she disappeared again he came obsessively to search for her each day. Until, on New Year's Eve, he came to the lake by moonlight, and she re-appeared. She too, it transpired, was in love with him. In fairy-tales such things happen. The result, (with folk-lore's characteristic staccato jump from cause to effect which leaves so much unexplained), was that they got married.

It was, however, a mixed marriage — mortal and immortal conjoining in a mortal world. She made him a single condition: if he ever struck her three times, she would go back. Some versions of the story have it that this separation must occur if he should strike her three times with iron, a detail which may or may not refer to the coming to South Wales of the metal-working Celts.

There is a catch, of course, and eventually he strikes her the three blows without being aware that that is what he is doing; tapping her, for instance, on the shoulder, to attract her attention. The familiar theme of the literal application of a term, which troubles the world of folklore, determines the outcome of the tale. She goes back into the lake.

The three blows have, however, occurred over a period of many years. And during this the two had produced a family of three sons. These, missing their mother, gravitate to the shores of Llyn-y-Fan Fach in the hopes of her return. One day she came, and subsequently on several occasions she emerged to meet and talk to her sons. During these times she taught them medicine, and the fame of the Physicians of Myddfai arises from this heritage. She gave them prescriptions and instructions, and took them to where the medicinal herbs grow in the valleys above Myddfai. The area bears in its topographical names some evidence of the ancientness of this tradition: Llidiad-y-Meddygon, gate of the physicians; Pant-y-Meddygon, physicians' valley.

The sons of the lake-maiden taught their sons the immortal cures, and for generations Myddfai turned out remarkable physicians. The lord of the manor of the area took a Myddfai doctor with him whenever he toured his territory; and the Lord Rhys gave them honours and privileges, a form of grant to encourage their work of healing the sick. Myddfai-originated doctors and others still claimed descent from them until the mid-nineteenth century, when the last of them appears to have died.

Llyn-y-Fan is now a reservoir, dammed and piped and under the care of the Llanelli Water Board. Presumably, since they were immortals, the lake-maiden and her kind are still there, under its unrevealing surface. One wonders if the people of Llanelli are aware that they have a woman living in their drinking water.

The book of the cures of the Physicians of Myddfai is a medieval manuscript at present in the British Museum. It contains some simple elements of folk-wisdom, and some fairly obvious truisms. You are advised not to eat too much at night. Some complicated natural mixtures are recommended for the curing of such things as warts, and several of their prescriptions, with overtones of magic, seem to have the same reference to the impossible as the trick of putting salt on a hen's tail. First take the tongue out of a live frog . . .

Myddfai today, in the northern, lower farming area of the Black Mountain's foothills, is a small village of some charm in the middle of lush countryside. Not far away, over the hills, is the Usk reservoir. The walk up to Llyn-y-Fan Fach is best made from the higher village of Llanddeusant, from where one can approach it now by narrow lanes winding between high hedges. And indeed the original physicians, if they were in the habit of walking frequently from Myddfai to the lake, could well have thought that a recipe for healthiness was the custom of taking exercise.

The Black Mountain, with its two Fans, lies to the west of the road which runs down, past the Cray reservoir, from Sennybridge to Ystradgynlais. The other side of this is the area known as Fforest Fawr, formerly the Great Forest of Brecknock, a royal hunting land which was the possession of the Crown during the Middle Ages. On both sides the long open slopes are reminiscent of the Scottish Highlands; there is the same feeling of ample space. The smooth-sided cwms

The Black Mountains near Crickhowell

and concave valley-slopes which the ice-age scraped out of the sandstone strata give the line of the horizon an elegance unknown to sharper and more brittle geomorphology. The area has a long tradition of sheep farming – even when it was supposedly a forest flocks grazed its open spaces – and the effect perhaps shows pervasively in the closely sheep-cropped grasses of its slopes. Today the hills bleat as strongly as ever, and mountain farmers on local ponies rodeo their flocks.

The Tawe river, which flows out at Swansea, rises in this valley above Glyntawe. As it then cuts deeper into the valley something about the nature of the place quite suddenly and distinctly changes. It is a move into limestone country, and while the plateaux and scarps, smooth slopes and long even ridges become impossible, features such as caves, quarries and waterfalls take their place.

In this characteristically complex and detailed valley sits the slightly monstrous bulk of Craig-y-Nos Castle, a large house, now a hospital, which was the home of the almost legendary soprano, Adelina Patti. Mme Patti was an Italian, born in Madrid, who made her operative debut in New York, at the age of seven. With such an international background it is perhaps not so surprising to find her marrying her second husband, an Italian tenor, in Swansea, in 1886. Signor Nicolini died in 1898, and the next year she was married again, this time in the Catholic Church at Brecon, to Baron Rolf Cederstrom who was more than 20 years her junior. Patti had bought Craig-y-Nos in 1878, and lived there until she died in 1919. It was a grand place at the time, with two lakes and a winter garden (the latter now transferred to Swansea, to become the Patti Pavilion), and was said to be the first private house to have electricity. It also had its own theatre, designed as a miniature of Drury Lane, in which Patti played the part of La Traviata, on its opening night in 1891.

The plain hillsides above Craig-y-Nos successfully disguise an amazing limestone accident which lies behind them. There is no clue that some miles of high vaulted tunnels lead into the hill.

The Dan-yr-Ogof cave complex was only discovered in 1912. Caves are not by any means scarce in the neighbourhood, and several major ones were already quite well known.

The Mountain Centre, Brecon
Tal-y-Bont Reservoir

Dan-y-Ogof had avoided discovery for so long because its natural entrance was small and high in the wall of the gorge through which the river Llynfell emerges from its underground life. The caves now are easily accessible, and with their length and roominess make an ideal and quite impressive tourist attraction. There is, however, something lacking. No primal paintings figure their rocks. No natural gaudy colours either, or unimagined textures, startle one in their formations. There is something about stalactites which is extremely tedious, only, perhaps, being exceeded by the greater futility of stalagmites. How could nature, normally so intemperate and immodest, take so many million years to achieve something so insignificant?

The river Twrch comes down from the Black Mountain mass to join the Tawe river near Ystradgynlais; and its name brings echoes again of the *Mabinogion*, in which the boar Twrch Trwyth was hunted by Arthur and his men from Ireland to Dyfed, from Dyfed into Ceredigion, and thence towards Gwent.

> Twrch Trwyth went then between Tawy and Ewyas. Arthur summoned Cornwall and Devon to meet him at the mouth of the Severn. And Arthur said to the warriors of this Island: "Twrch Trwyth has slain many of my men. By the valour of men, not while I am alive shall he go into Cornwall."

The boar himself finally eluded the Emperor by swimming out to sea; and no-one knows where he eventually landed. The river which bears his name comes down a wooded valley between humped, gritty hills and the outcrops of coal-tips. It flows out of the world of unchanged, untouched wilderness, scarps and mountain lakes well able to be the homes of immortal maidens; and down past Ystradgynlais into the world of antiseptic modern housing and ambitious highway schemes.

VIII   BRECON

Standing today on Pen-y-Crug one gets a view which is largely
dominated by the field pattern, with its associated well-
established hedgerow trees, that trellis-work of lines forming
irregular squares and rectangles which, because they are so
universal on our valley slopes, go almost without notice. The
residue of a medieval cultivation system, combined with the
effects of the Enclosures. The tree-line however defines itself,
and a moment's lapse into illusion can re-instate the tangled
forests which, when the Romans came to Brecon, enabled the
Silures to resist their domination for a generation.

The Crug (as they call it) is a high, round hill, almost
conical, rising to over a thousand feet, overlooking the
hollow in which Brecon itself sits by the Usk. It was
defended by a considerable series of earthworks, probably by
the invading metal-working Celtic-speaking peoples, probably
during the second half of the first millennium B.C. Five
ramparts in all encircle it; and its extensive size implies a
considerable population. Not only would they not have made
it so big if there had not been many of them, but it would
have taken many of them to make it at all. It is a fine spot,
with a wide view over the surrounding country, and the
ramparts and ditches are still clearly in place.

The tribe on the Crug were not the first people to inhabit
Brecon. There are, as everywhere in the district, cromlechs
and barrows not too far away. Lake-dwellers dwelt on an
artificially-constructed island in nearby Llangorse lake,
although such villages have sometimes turned out to be of
comparatively late dates. But Pen-y-Crug would seem to
represent, in a clear form, the first large, organized settlement
of Brecon.

The Romans came into the area in the 70s, A.D. The great
invasion of South Wales probably took place during the years
74 and 75, and it would be at this period that they built,

along with several other major forts, the great military establishment of Brecon Gaer. The Gaer is the largest of the second-level, auxiliary forts, in Wales. It was garrisoned by Spanish cavalry, and remained in use until the end of the second century. The gateways and walls which can be seen were probably part of a renovation which took place about 140. The fort was occupied again when the army briefly returned at the beginning of the third century A.D. And it was empty again by the end of that century, never to be properly restored to military use. There is some evidence that attempts were made to refortify it a long time later, but in an inexpert way which suggests a temporary panic rather than a strategy.

Brecon after that has little history until the arrival of the Normans, with their feudal lordships and their castles. Brecon's was one of the earliest of these, being established in 1094, by Bernard Newmarch, no less than the Conqueror's half-brother. The original castle was considerably enlarged under succeeding Normans, one of whom, Humphry de Bohun, granted the town its charter in the 1270s.

The motte of the old castle can be seen above the river Honddu, a tower-topped mound standing in the Bishop's garden under the Cathedral. Some fine walls stand, separated from this by the road which comes down the hill, in the gardens of the Castle Hotel, to give a clue as to the considerable size of the full structure. But most of the castle had long ago been taken down; it was destroyed, in fact, by the people of Brecon themselves, in order to avoid the involvement in the Civil Wars which so many castled towns around them suffered.

Much more splendid than these ruins, and in part almost as old, is the church of St John the Evangelist, now the Cathedral of the Diocese of Swansea and Brecon. The Benedictine Priory which grew up beside the càstle and walled town was founded, like the town, by Bernard Newmarch. Probably there was already a church on the spot, one of the humbler structures which, during the twelfth and thirteenth centuries, were translated into stone. Most of the present building belongs to the thirteenth and fourteenth centuries, but possibly some early features remain from the

original foundation. The font, for instance, a sturdily round
bowl with a pattern of Celtic intertwining strands running
around its edge, may be left over from the early twelfth-
century church which Newmarch founded. The church
interior is largely in the Early English style, the chancel, with
its deeply-set tall lancets, being earlier than the nave.

Outside, the Cathedral among its trees looks imposing and
bulkily majestic. Monastic buildings to its south were
restored and given to the diocese (having, after the
Dissolution, fallen into private hands) in 1925. They now
form the Deanery and Chapter House; and the whole – a
religious conclave of fine and secluded buildings, properly
dominated by its tall Cathedral – is enclosed by high
battlemented walls, a rare example of a fortified religious
domain.

It is hard to forget, at any point, Brecon's connection with
the army. As a depot of the South Wales Borderers (now
merged into the Royal Regiment of Wales), whose barracks,
with its Regimental Museum, is on the edge of the town on
the road out to Abergavenny, the place has been dominated,
and still is, by a military presence. The regiment's Memorial
Chapel occupies a corner of the Cathedral.

Brecon in its hollow, its tall buildings enclosing narrow
streets, does not give itself to views, either of itself or out of
it, from its main streets. But one only has to go a short way
down the Promenade, which leads abruptly out of the town
centre and into open country, or up above the castle into the
area of well-spaced housing on the slope above the Usk, to
get the full impact of that classic scenic skyline. The Beacons
rise, ridged and moulded, one beside the other. Between
them and the Promenade stretches rolling green country,
with the river Usk underlining it.

Brecon Promenade, rightly an object of pride, is a thickly
treelined avenue running beside the river. It leads to the
several items of recreation which the town possesses,
bowling, boating, putting, paddling. Sedate and undemanding, it is the sort of rural amble which is the ideal
complement to a town.

Brecon has been traditionally a centre of the woollen
industry; and in fact a wool factory still exists there, by the

river, today. During the age of the expansion of communications the town became linked to the world both by road
and canal. The Monmouthshire canal, which runs from
Newport via Pontypool and Abergavenny, has its terminus at
Brecon, where it draws water from the Usk. It lies almost
motionless, small and muddy-brown, along the south-east
corner of the town. In the 1750s the stage-coach had come,
providing a contact with London itself. Brecon was never
really a backwater, and yet never quite the centre of affairs.

In spite of its ancientness and its well-concentrated,
nuclear layout, it is not a visually distinguished town. The
architecture (and to a large extent the population) tends to
be noticeably mixed. Its present-day importance is perhaps as
a centre for the Brecon Beacons National Park.

The Park was designated in 1957, at which time it was in
three separate counties, and consequently administered by
park planning committees of their three county councils,
with that ambiguously placed co-ordinating body, a joint
advisory committee. Unlike most Parks it has not now
benefited by local government reorganization; it became
divided between four authorities instead of three. A joint
committee, drawn from the county councils of all four
counties, with its own Park Officer, now administers it.
Though this is an improvement on the powerless position of
the joint advisory committee, it still leaves the danger that
Park affairs may take second place, in the priorities of its
administrators, to other county matters and demands.

Its rather unsatisfactory background situation, however,
seems to have done it remarkably little harm, and it has to a
large extent escaped the pressures and intrusions which other
Parks, nearer to the densely populated areas and the main
lines of communication, have unfortunately suffered. Very
much of its total of 500 square miles remains undamaged. In
few places in Britain is the landscape so much due not to the
effect of human land-use but to events of millions of years
before such things became a possibility. The Brecon Beacons
are related most directly to the time when the shallow seas
began to dry, where the Beacons now are, and to reveal the
deposits which had been gradually laid down beneath them.

Old Red Sandstone belongs to the Devonian series of

rocks, and as it occurs in the Brecon Beacons it contains a number of subdivisions. Of these – such types as Red Marls, Brownstones, Tilestones – some are more resistant than others, and the most resistant, Brownstones topped by Plateau Beds of conglomerates and coarse brown sandstones, are those which have remained at the most elevated places. In fact the summit of the Beacons, Pen-y-Fan, is the highest Old Red Sandstone summit in Britain, as well as being the highest peak in South Wales.

One of the great successes of the Park (with its task of mediating between the landscape and the public) must surely be the Mountain Centre, visited by hundreds for refreshment and information, a well-proportioned building set squarely on the foothills of the Beacons near Libanus, which, if it did nothing else, would illustrate the effect which architectural design can have on the atmosphere of a building. The Mountain Centre has an air of calmness and decency which induces a feeling of ease. It was opened in 1966, and caters with willingness and enthusiasm for walkers, archaeologists, bus-loads of children, foreign tourists, and people who want nothing more than somewhere to sit undisturbed and enjoy the graceful view and the mild air.

Several roads run through the Beacons and through Fforest Fawr, all more or less in a north-south direction. Ponies and their foals sip at the dew-ponds (not wild, but turned out onto the hills in summer, like the sheep) and everywhere the gentle contours of the sandstone gives long, soft sweeping slopes which in their turn produce a relaxing mood: unhurried, unstrained. The Merthyr road runs down past reservoirs, in the Taf Fawr valley, down to the sprawling outskirts of Merthyr Tydfil. From it a lane crosses wilder country, back again, up the Taf Fechan valley from Cefn-Coed. Reservoirs again lie either side of the ridge which it crosses, coming down back to the Usk valley at Talybont.

Here in the Taf Fechan and Talybont valleys the forestry plantations to some extent accentuate the open flanks of the mountains above them. But in some places there is no doubt that the conifers have crept too far up onto those splendid, sweeping slopes. There are areas around the heads of the valleys where planting has been effective in covering the scars of the mining era. But one should not let its usefulness in places disguise its overwhelmingly transforming effect in others. If a thing is recognized as good, as, for instance, the scenery in a National Park is as it were classified as officially good, then there is a prima facie argument for not changing it at all. To change it, therefore, one would need to show some overriding reason, and this can hardly be said to have been done. The total physical change effected by the forests is such a radical and complete, and permanent, metamorphosis of the countryside, that one begins to wonder how it can ever have been thought compatible with the presumably protective intentions behind calling somewhere a National Park.

The Forestry Commission has made efforts, at a very late date, to mitigate its antisocial actions (blocking off views, restricting walking, driving out much of the flora and fauna of the hills) by the provision of forest nature trails and picnic sites. Diversification may perhaps eventually lead to a decrease of its enormous annual loss; and if tourism is a major profit-making industry (which timber is evidently not) then the Commission would clearly be wise to turn its attention to further expansion in this direction, from trees to tourists. The social benefits in the form of relief of pressure, the absorption, out of sight, of cars, and tents, and caravans, could compensate in part, at least, for the coniferization of the scenery.

To some extent paralleling this lane across the Talybont, a minor road runs up the Senni valley, to the west of the main Merthyr road, joining the branch running down to Hirwaun, at Penderyn. The climb out of the Senni valley is spectacular, the narrow road snaking up by hairpin bends, to run between the highest points of Fforest Fawr. And over the empty hills and down to Ystradfellte. Here it breaks into the limestone belt, and the gorges choked with indigenous scrub break the view into patches and clusters, pieces of valleys glimpsed round corners. Sandstone scenery is simple; wide sweeps of unmarked and even slope. Limestone land is all blocks and breaks and little rivers.

Two typical rivers, the Mellte and the Hepste, converge near Ystradfellte. Most famous of their features, perhaps, is

Cyfarthfa Castle
Caerphilly Castle (overleaf)
Aberfan Community Centre (overleaf)

Sgwd-yr-Eira, a waterfall whose white curtain often lives up to its attractive name: fall of snow. Ledges of sandstone have resisted the erosion of the water, which has washed away the softer shales at its base, the result of which is that it is possible to cross the Hepste behind the curtain of the fall. This effective gimmick can be easily reached by a farm track leading from the corner of Penderyn village, providing that, when the track forks, one takes the lower, right-hand branch. The fall only performs properly when the river is full of water, and can be disappointing in a drought.

Sgwd-yr-Eira is only one of the many tricks of the Hepste and the Mellte. Just downstream of it the Hepste, for instance, runs largely underground, to emerge gurgling in a deep green pool. And this is nothing. The Mellte flows below a mainly dry bed for a mile, near Ystradfellte; and at Porth-yr-Ogof it goes off into the hill through the mouth of a cave, and reappears, delighted with its joke, in a gorge a little further down. Below Sgwd-yr-Eira the Hepste runs under some towering block-formed cliffs of a spectacular small gorge. The clustering trees and the roar of the water make it a place of prime romantic beauty.

From Brecon the Usk flows east, and beside it flow both the canal and the Abergavenny road. The canal, creeping along the hillside under overhanging trees, and now and then emerging, as at Talybont, to become a part of the village scene, encounters the river and the minor road at several points, being put to the need to resort to tunnels and viaducts, and doggedly continues, quiet and unobtrusive, along the sloping hillside on its way to Abergavenny.

Near Talybont itself, with its swing-bridge over the canal, is the small church of Llansantffraid, across the valley on the other side of the Usk. The comparatively modern church is of little interest, but it occupies the site of an earlier one, and it was there, in 1695, that the poet Henry Vaughan was buried.

Vaughan boasted of his South Wales identity, calling himself the Silurist, and the Swan of Usk. His family had property in the valley nearby, and as a consequence he became, on leaving Oxford, a country doctor in the Usk valley. Vaughan is best known for his deeply-felt religious poetry, which succeeds almost in conveying the obscure

experience of ecstasy; but it was not until 1650, after his first
two volumes of poetry had been writtten, that he underwent
a religious conversion, following an illness. Thereafter his
verse became infused with the strong spirituality which the
diction of his time serves to express in so clear and forceful
a way. Much of the intense and gleaming style, which he
shares with his contemporaries Marvell and Lovelace, is
derived from the influence of their predecessor George
Herbert. But it is perhaps, of all these, Vaughan himself who
comes over most immediately and emotively to us today.

> I saw eternity the other night
> Like a great ring of pure and endless light,
>   All calm, as it was bright;
> And round beneath it, Time in hours, days, years,
>   Driven by the spheres
> Like a vast shadow moved, in which the world
>   And all her train were hurled.

The feeling is as rich as the valley out of which it came.
The Usk runs from Brecon to Crickhowell through fertile
farmland, flat arable fields along the valley bottom complementing the healthy dairy pastures all around. The whole-
someness of it all is overpowering. So much fecundity, so
much wealth.

Down at Crickhowell the view changes slightly; Abergavenny's Sugar Loaf mountain shows its back, to the east,
and to the north one long solitary limestone outcrop, Pen
Cerrig Calch, limestone even to the name, cuts into Brecon's
sandstone area. Crickhowell lies near its old bridge over the
river, while the canal, on the opposite bank of the valley,
loops around the contour to avoid any disturbance to its
calm inertia.

Up to the north of Crickhowell the Black Mountains
stretch, another large and open extent of smooth slopes and
wide views. They eventually pitch down to the Vale of
Ewyas, where another Honddu river runs through Llanthony
and Capel-y-Ffin; an area, like that of Abergavenny, visited in
a later chapter. To the west of the Black Mountains mass the
land falls in sloping agricultural acres to provide the shallow

dip in which sits Llangorse lake.

This sheet of water, nowhere very deep, in its slight hollow of farmland, is well-known, and rightly, for its beauty. Its reedy shores and its wide extent make it reminiscent, in patches, of the Norfolk Broads. Legends of a drowned town under its waters can hardly have any validity, but may perhaps refer to a dim memory that at one time, within the period of human habitation, the lake was not there. If that was so it must have been very long ago, as is implied by the existence of the crannog, or artificial island, built by lake-dwellers out of wooden piles, now a reedy inlet at the northern side of the water.

The beauty of this lovely stretch of water is not spoilt, but rather emphasized or set in context, by the sails of yachts and the ripples of rowing-boats; any more than the view of its banks is spoit by the field-patterns of the dotted farms. The lake is heavily used for recreation. It has been found, however, that some forms of recreation are not compatible with others, and there is a strong case for the prohibition of the use of motor boats and water skis. The ecology of the lake and its banks is easily upset, and since it provides considerable interest not only for anglers but for naturalists of all kinds, this point is important.

Brecon is fortunate (lacking easy access to the sea) to have this large area of water near at hand. It completes the set of the area's considerable attractions. Mountains, valleys, rivers, villages and country towns. That so much of such high quality should be packed into reach of a small radius from the town of Brecon is, perhaps, only another example of the variety and scope which South Wales has to offer.

PART FOUR

THE VALLEYS

IX TAFF

'Merthyr' means martyr. 'Tydfil' is the name of a saint. 'Merthyr Tydfil' means South Welsh industrialism, social degradation, political unrest.

The valleys of South Wales have become overlaid with more than their share of associated images, and so strong is the picture that it is hard even for experienced people to free them, in their minds, from coal-dust and hymn-singing, whippets, beer-drinking, chapel-going and squalid backyards. Some reputations spread more easily than others, and South Wales as a whole has undoubtedly come under the cloud of this largely illusory and certainly historically isolated picture.

Much of the country, even the coal-mining area, seems in real life to be specifically designed to disillusion. In South Wales, in fact, it is quite hard to find a coal-mine, and there is not all that much singing. Here and there, no doubt, it is possible to find a choir at practice. The diligent traveller will no doubt be able to track down leprechauns in Ireland, where everybody constantly, of course, says "Begorrah". Very often a country becomes best known for doing what it hardly ever does. Indeed several great choirs are still in stalwart existence, and one would certainly not wish to deny that Welshmen sing enthusiastically at Rugby matches; nor that, in the occasional dingy bar, a little man in a cap can be found in a corner giving a reedy, lonely solo —

> So close your — eyes
> My little — drummer-boy . . .

But as a whole, in their normal lives, South Welshmen do not often find themselves singing.

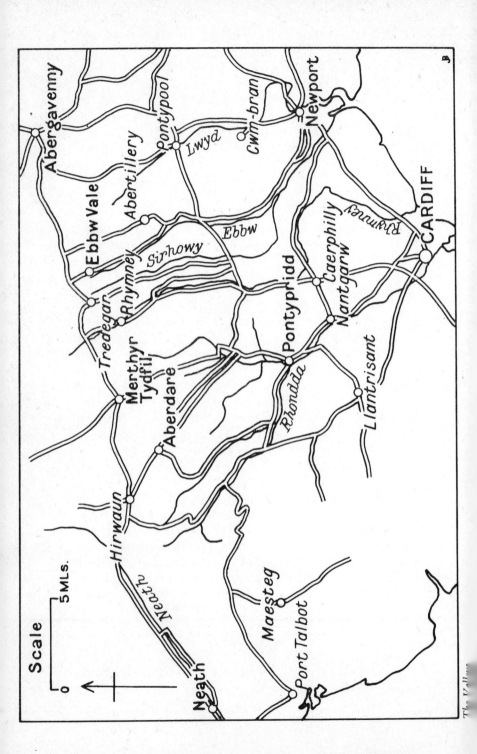

Scale

5 MLS.

0

Abergavenny

Ebbw Vale

Abertillery

Pontypool

Lwyd

Cwm-bran

Newport

CARDIFF

Rhymney

Sirhowy

Ebbw

Rhymney

Caerphilly

Tredegar

Merthyr
Tydfil

Aberdare

Pontypridd

Nantgarw

Rhondda

Llantrisant

Hirwaun

Neath

Maesteg

Port Talbot

Neath

The Valleys

B

Coal-mines, however, definitely do not dominate, now, even the Valleys. And there is a historical sense in which they never really did. Industry of various sorts has played a big part in the history of this small area; but the hills themselves, spaciously rearing over the cramped valley bottom, were, and remain, the major feature of the landscape.

Historically it really all begins at Merthyr. A classic combination of international events, geological contingencies, and personal characteristics, made what was, up to 1760, a small collection of cottages on a wild hillside, into the largest and most important town in Wales, in a mere hundred years.

The first furnace opened in 1759, and the next year John Guest, (whose name has since run through Welsh mineral industry to reach an end in 'Guest, Keen and Nettlefolds'), was employed to manage it. Guest came from Shropshire, which was also an iron-working district. Indeed none of the early iron-masters were of Welsh origin. In the four first iron-works of the Merthyr area, Guest at Dowlais and Homfray at first Penydarren and then Plymouth were both Shropshire men; and Crawshay at Cyfarthfa came from Yorkshire. Likewise the population which the new industry at Merthyr rapidly attracted came partly from the iron-working counties of Shropshire and Staffordshire, and partly, because the area still completely lacked road, from the parts of the county within reasonable reach, such as Gloucestershire and the West Country and nearby parts of rural Wales.

The term of Guest's early management at the Dowlais works coincided with wars with France, which created a demand for munitions which in turn led to a growing need for iron. His first major step was to switch the industry from burning charcoal to burning coke. Both were ready at hand, but the forests were becoming rapidly depleted, and, although he could hardly have foreseen it, the coal available in the area was so plentiful that it would be hard for it ever to run short.

At that time there were no roads in the Valleys. Rough tracks ran up from Cardiff, and down them went the iron and coal on the backs of pack ponies. In 1767, however, the first roads began to be constructed. In 1789 was formed the South Wales Association for the Improvement of Roads. By the end of the century the major benefit of four canals was added. One from Brecon via Abergavenny and Pontypool terminated at Newport; one from Merthyr, with a branch to Aberdare, ran down to Cardiff. And with these two connections the possibility of the expansion of the two ports came about, since they were now linked to the iron-works. Another ran from the Neath river to a point near Hirwaun, and the fourth joined the Swansea valley to the port at Swansea.

In 1780 activity in the war with America was renewed, and the fresh demand for cannons led to increasing business at Merthyr. In 1793 further wars with France coincided with the rise to power, at Merthyr, of Richard Crawshay, who was to found, at the Cyfarthfa works, a dynasty as powerful as Guest's. From then on, until, towards the end of the century, the iron and steel industry gave way to coal and the Merthyr area became eclipsed by the expansion of the Rhondda, the town boomed. It boomed like a gold-rush town, hectically and euphorically. The population of the county borough was, in the 1960s, some ten thousand people fewer than the population of the Merthyr valley in the 1860s. It grew from 7,700 in 1801 to 69,618 in 1861, and with this devastating transformation came, of course, the roots of dangerous social problems.

Two technical innovations had taken place during the 1780s, combining with the American wars to make Merthyr a node of progress. Watt's improved steam engine led both to a new form of transport for iron and coal and to a new demand for them both. At the same time the invention of puddling, producing wrought iron, overcame some of the troubles which, with cast iron, had tended to hold the industry back. And in this new technique in particular Cyfarthfa led the way. It only required the canals, then the tramroads, then the railways, to open up Merthyr's full potential.

The industry received a set-back, or a pause in its soaring expansion, in the 1850s, when the invention of steel, which proved to be more use than iron in the making of subsequent railroads, faced it with enormous problems. Penydarren closed in 1858, and Hirwaun in 1859. In 1890 Rhymney turned to coal-production. Blaenavon and Cyfarthfa survived

Newport Transporter Bridge

at Merthyr into the next century. Cyfarthfa had changed to making steel in 1884, and Dowlais (under the enthusiastic leadership of Sir John Guest, grandson of the first manager) even earlier; but, as we have seen, the geographical position of Merthyr, now that local ores were unsuitable for use, had given rise to an unacceptable increase in costs. Dowlais moved to the coast in 1891, and in 1910 Cyfarthfa closed.

By 1860, however, most of the railways were finished (though in a smaller way they continued to be built, of course, into the 1870s and well beyond). The coalfields had been leased to the iron companies on 99-year leases, and these were now, a hundred years after John Guest's arrival in the Merthyr area, beginning to run out. They were renewed by their aristocratic owners at vastly greater prices, making the production of coal not just an insignificant side-effect of the business of fuelling an iron foundry, but a major undertaking in itself. At the same time, as we have seen, the demand for it for its own sake had been increasing. The age of the iron-masters was about to be replaced by that of the coal kings.

In the area itself the building of railways, which had given rise to only a finite amount of demand for iron, provided a continuing need for quantities of coal for fuel. Taking it as a small sample of what went on elsewhere, one can see that the actual construction period was over, and the consumption period therefore in full form, by 1860. In 1850 Brunel's South Wales Railway, (to be linked to his Great Western by the building of Chepstow Bridge in 1852), had joined Chepstow to Swansea. It continued to Aberdare in 1850, and in 1853 the South Wales Railway extended to Merthyr itself. Rhondda coal travelled by railway to Cardiff for the first time in 1855. The line continued through the Rhondda valley in 1856. In 1858 the Rhymney valley likewise joined the network.

After the 1860s Merthyr began to decline. It had occasional bouts of rejuvenation, but these finally came to an end in the '20s and '30s of this century, and some 13,000 people removed themselves from its population statistics during the 20 years following 1930. What are we left with now? The iron industry bequeathed to us its slag heaps and

Castell Coch

derelict land. Its other heritage of old, substandard cottages has proved much easier to remove, and in any case less absorbing of the valuable valley space. Its population, in spite of all vicissitudes, has been remarkably enduring. It stands, during the 1970s, at somewhere around 60,000.

Possibly because of the proximity of Herefordshire, possibly because of the border and West Country origins of the population, here, as quite often in the upper valleys, the people have a partly western English identity, symptoms of which show in the thick soft accent and the pronounced taste for rough cider.

A pleasant shopping town, now supported by new industries. The old squalor has gone. The crumbling and resentful streets of outworn cottages have been swept away, leaving Merthyr incredibly intact, its spirit and self-awareness instantly recognizable. It is a strong-natured town, confident and purposeful in a way that makes one feel that far from looking to London as its capital it hardly even looks to Cardiff. Merthyr is the capital of the Taff valley, and in spite of the troubles and struggles of its history (or perhaps because of them) there is something in its make-up which is not destructible. A brand new town centre now replaces the gutted area of the old town; the Hoover factory in the Taff valley provides well-paid employment for more than 5,000 people; and there is, overall, a prosperous and cheerful feeling about the town.

Even Cyfarthfa Castle, once the palace of the Crawshays, now the property of the town and a museum and art gallery, is not as grotesque or pretentious as one would expect. It was early among industrial mock-castles, and seems to have been done with less megalomania and more taste than most.

It is hard to relate the historical facts surrounding names such as Crawshay and Cyfarthfa to the reality of Merthyr today. What we see now is a town in the process of undergoing some sort of rebirth. The new buildings are bright and lively, stylish without being at all aggressive. Certainly on the immediate outskirts of the shopping centre slag heaps the size of mountains rear over the town. A few old terraces at the top of the town show what it must have been like. But social character of the area, however, has not greatly changed; the population is one class only, manual workers. There are no middle-class housing areas or middle-class jobs.

Smaller family units, now, as well as the increase of the new population, have led to a demand for yet more housing. The terraces, even when modernized, are not always up to the standards which the times now demand. They lack, for instance, anywhere to put a car. Based on the assumption that work was within walking distance, they are not always located as pleasantly or as conveniently as are the new estates. The latter operate the reverse assumption; such places as that above the Rhonddas, with its steep slopes and its distance from shops or work places, rely entirely on the car.

Of the many distinctive features of coal-mining as an industry, one which most concerned South Wales was the effect of the location of the material. It forced people to live, in vast numbers, in this mountainous terrain, isolated from normal settlements and other ways of life. In South Wales too the type of coal was significant, and the evolution of the industry involved a shift west, towards the Rhondda, and a movement higher up the valleys.

The use of coal was not, of course, an innovation of the nineteenth century. It had, like most things, been used by the ancient Chinese, the Greeks, and finally the Romans. Coal-mining in Britain probably started after the Norman Conquest, and cannot be traced back reliably beyond the thirteenth century. For domestic purposes people preferred to burn timber, which caused less pollution in the form of smoke and fumes. But during the sixteenth century wood began to become more of a scarce commodity, and London already, by then, had started buying Newcastle coal.

Had it continued to be a question of domestic hearths, the coal-mining industry might never have changed much from its slow and even development over that century and the next. It was, of course, the Industrial Revolution which radically revised the picture.

The change of demand from smokeless fuel (which Londoners were bringing from South Wales in 1830) of the central valleys area, to dry-steam and anthracite further west, arose from the increasing use of coal, during that century, for fuelling steam-powered factories rather than for heating houses. Britain was not the only country to become industrialized, but benefited from the beginning from its anticipation of the process. The export to France formed the mainstay of the early coal industry. The steamship companies expanded during the 1860s, and by 1881, as we have seen, Cardiff was the biggest coal-exporter in the world.

At first most of the coal came from the Aberdare and Rhymney valleys. The lower Rhondda, being connected to Cardiff by train in 1855, started the next wave of coal-production. The Upper Rhondda began to be developed from 1864. By 1870 there were 5,000 miners there, producing nearly two million tons a year. The higher wages which the profitable new industry offered drew workers from Merthyr, and contributed to the already inevitable decline of the one place and expansion of the other. From the '60s onwards both Merthyr and Aberdare had largely static populations, and it was the time of the western coalfields and the ports.

Coal is cheap to export. Economies of scale apply, so that larger boats give cheaper transport costs per ton. The average tonnage of vessels therefore went up, and freight rates correspondingly went down. In 1850 the average tonnage of vessels at Cardiff was 1,000. By 1880 it had multiplied by three, and coal freight costs per ton were halved between 1872 and the end of the century. Exports thus began to form the bulk of production. Following the sudden boom of the Rhondda fields, exports of coal went up between the 1860s and the 1880s from 1.7 million tons per year to 9.2.

All this had happened very fast, and it was bound to have results of a social, as well as an economic kind. Large numbers of people, a mixed-background population, the effects of uprooting and placing in strange surroundings: purely social consequences interacted and combined with the physical ones of hard work and bad conditions. Housing conditions could never, have been really adequate. The houses (however strong and well-built they look to us today) were very hastily erected, with little forethought or plan. The narrowness of the valleys and the lack of space on the valley floor restricted what was possible. There was, moreover, desperate overcrowding; taking in lodgers was a common practice, although many of the cottages had only two bedrooms and were already full of large families. Shift-sleeping was also resorted to widely, as a natural consequence of shift-working and lack of bed-space.

Drainage and health requirements in general became a severe problem at an early stage. Merthyr was the archetype of this effect on hygiene of sudden urban growth, and was criticized for its bad conditions by health reports in 1845, 1850, 1853, and 1870. But there was, of course, by then not much that could be done.

With these factors came, at an early point, the first rumblings of trouble. In 1799 the Combination Laws made workers' associations illegal, but meetings continued secretly nevertheless. Terrorist gangs, such as the infamous 'Scotch Cattle', enforced the regulations of the 'lodges'. Repressive legislation, by forcing the workers to take the law into their own hands, had proved counterproductive.

In 1824 the Combination Laws were repealed, but strikes were still illegal. Striking then led to rioting and the use of troops, and by the 1830s the ulterior motives of forming Unions (which had been first intended for mutual assistance in hard times) began to be recognized. Known Union leaders were sacked from their jobs in 1831. There was rioting in Merthyr in that year, in which twenty people were killed and sixty wounded; the ringleader was hanged at Cardiff.

The Unions were not rich enough to sustain strikes, and it became clear that such civil methods of arbitrating between the power of the iron-masters and the dissatisfaction of the workers was inadequate. Pressure for Parliamentary Reform began.

The first Reform Act of 1832 was a disappointment. What difference, after all, did the giving of the franchise to 'ten pound householders' make to the workers of Merthyr? In 1832 Merthyr became, under the Reform Act, a Parliamentary Borough. But the new middle-class electorate naturally elected J. J. Guest, the current iron-master, so that the power remained exactly where it was before.

Disturbances continued, and workers who were willing to co-operate with employers were coerced by workers from other areas. Confrontation led to near-stoppages of the iron industry in 1834, in which year the new Poor Law also fell far short of providing a remedy for the ills of the situation.

The movement which arose out of this early trade unionism was called 'Chartist' because of its proposal (in 1838) for the institution of a People's Charter. In 1839 there was a Chartist riot at Llanidloes, in mid-Wales, at which prisoners were freed from the jail and the police were beaten. An abortive follow-up to this took place at Newport, where a Chartist demonstration of about 5,000 men ended in failure and marked the end, in that form, of Welsh Chartism. The leaders were transported.

It is strange to find, in this harsh social climate, that the wife of Merthyr's new M.P., J. J. Guest, (who became in 1838 the first baronet, Sir John, and was the grandson of the first John Guest of Dowlais), was none other than that talented and civilized woman, Lady Charlotte Guest.

Lady Charlotte seems to have been a very remarkable person. Daughter of the Earl of Lindsey, she married Guest in 1833. During the next ten years or so she not only learnt to understand Welsh, but became one of the language's major scholars. She translated the stories collected in the Red Book of Hergest, a manuscript, at present in the library of Jesus College, Oxford, dating from the end of the fourteenth century. To the elegant and atmospheric translation of these old Welsh stories, which she published in 1846, she gave the title *Mabinogion*. The word in itself is a mistaken version of the plural of '*mabinogi*', which she understood to mean 'a tale of youth'. The work as a whole has proved to be, without doubt, a most influential event in British literature. It opened people's eyes to the existence of a whole new literary world.

Besides this achievement of scholarship and art, Lady Charlotte also found time to occupy herself with an attempt to improve the area she lived in. She founded schools, for instance, at Dowlais and Merthyr Tydfil.

The 1840s then saw a slight improvement in conditions, but unrest continued elsewhere under a different form. The Rebecca riots of that period were more a question of the urban dissatisfaction spreading to the countryside. They had as their target the toll-road system, which was a burden to farmers, and their leader took the pseudonym of Rebecca from the somewhat obscure Biblical text of Genesis 24, verse 60. "And they blessed Rebecca, and said unto her, Thou art our sister, be thou the mother of thousands of millions, and let thy seed possess the gate of those which hate them." This dispute over the possession of the gate reached some sort of outcome in 1844, when a commission of inquiry removed many of the turnpike grievances.

After the Second Reform Act in 1867 there was, politically, an upsurge of Liberalism, which was to be increased again by the Third Reform Act of 1884. We are now into the coal age and in the middle of the effects of the acceleration of economic and social factors. There was wage trouble accompanied by stoppages in the early 1870s. In 1875, however, prices were falling, and when coal prices fall it means that trade has dropped and there is less demand for labour. Power was thus moved into the hands of the employers and they had cut wages twice in 1874. A third proposed reduction in 1875 led to renewed conflict and in May of that year a sliding-scale was proposed which was to prove historically significant. It was the first attempt to settle an industrial dispute by negotiation rather than coercion.

Wages were tied, by the sliding-scale, to the selling price of coal. This removed, for the bosses, the constant danger of expensive labour conflict; and for the workers the insecurity of arbitrary and perhaps unnecessary wage-cuts. The principle was refined and improved during the 1870s and '80s. It failed, however, to give the the ultimate security, in the long-term, of a guaranteed minimum.

The sliding-scale did much to keep the always-present tension from reaching an eruption during the next two decades. In 1898 the South Wales Miners' Federation came into existence, and by 1909 the Eight Hours Act, treating miners for the first time, perhaps, as if they were human beings, ensured that they would have some free time.

Keir Hardie, in the meantime, had won the Merthyr constituency for the working classes, and thus set on its way the labour movement which was to become, by an inevitable historical progression, a major part of South Wales's cultural tradition.

Hardie was born in Lanarkshire in 1856. He was himself a miner, and first became politically active as the secretary to a miners' union. In 1892 he was elected to Parliament as Labour member for West Ham (south), and thus became the single member of the new party. He lost his seat in 1895, and failed for a time to get another. When he was voted in at Merthyr, in 1900, it proved a turning point. Now, with a safe seat, he was able to devote the remaining 15 years of his life to bantering Parliament into taking the fact of unemployment seriously, and to fostering the rise of the Independent Labour Party. This, in 1900, had formed the Labour Representative Committee, which six years later became the Labour Party, as it is today.

One feels the aftermath of all this now in what seems, sometimes, to be a dated set of concepts lingering among the physical remains, in the valleys, of these times. Certainly it is ideas, as much as structures, that have grown there, arisen out of contemporary needs and then stayed on. Inevitably with an accumulation of large numbers of people come not only the facilities which they require – housing, shops, chapels and inns – but also the ideas which they need to structure their joint lives. To have a working-men's club or institute, for instance (and without one a Valleys town would seem strangely incomplete), one first needs to have the idea of the working-man. The strength with which such things grew there, then and afterwards, is not only a function of hard conditions and poor pay. The area built on, in the Rhondda valley, contained by early this century a population density of 24,000 people per square mile, and none of them had their origins in the place. The fact allowed, as in other suddenly urbanized places, a complete break with the thinking of traditional English social structure. It also permitted a view of the social fact in isolation from any long period of evolution. Uprooted populations, people without a settled nature, are able to view themselves (as villagers and farmers are not) in the abstract: as 'the working class', 'the proletariat', 'the urban workers', 'the people'.

Meanwhile the sheep, above Treorchy, still graze the slopes, and much of the mountains over the Upper Rhondda have remained unaffected by what was, historically, a brief and isolated period of activity. Treorchy thrives as a shopping centre for the upper valley, where even now a population remains. But coal no longer dominates. In 1970 three collieries were left in the whole of the Rhondda, employing 3,500 people; 39,919 were employed in collieries in 1924.

The valleys in general now are not squalid, but lovely; green and airy places where everything is clean and bright. Acid soil over Pennant Sandstone provides rough grazing for sheep. The coal dust has settled and been washed away. The few remaining pits are dwarfed by their surroundings. The vast tips are grassed over or forested and now appear rather as an imaginative piece of landscaping than as the product of wholesale exploitation. The industry which provides current jobs for the remaining population is largely located on well-laid-out industrial estates (for instance between Hirwaun and Glyn Neath, at the top of the Upper Rhondda), and modern factories can often be an asset to the landscape rather than a detraction.

Neath itself, at the far west of the coalfield, is large and industrial, but is set in the middle of plentiful scenery; hills on one side, wooded slopes on another. The Neath valley below it is rich with deciduous trees.

The town of Neath is one of the oldest-established of the towns of the industrial belt. It occupies the site of the Roman field fort of Nidum, and possesses the rather sad remains of a castle built in 1300. It started copper smelting early in the eighteenth century. Ores came from Cardiganshire, metal-workers from Shropshire, and convict labour was used for the heavy work. The smelting took place at first in coal pits, and coal-reliant industries have continued to play an important part in Neath's development. Now it is a busy but not beautiful town, in constant tension between congestion and decay, its age showing in places, its long preoccupation with worldy affairs giving it lines of stress.

In contrast to the scrub-and-copse-clothed Neath valley, the Afan (or Avon) valley which runs in a similar direction, from the coalfield to the coast, a little further south, is luxurious, though not excessively, with conifers. The valleys both face towards Swansea Bay, but differ radically in type. That up from Port Talbot to Cwmavon is small and pretty, and what makes the slopes of it so pleasant now is the mixture of spruce and larch in the planting, a combination which gives a subtle and changing texture and colour to the terrain. The road runs up to the village of Cymmer, which is not to be confused with another Cymmer (the name, strictly with one 'm', means 'confluence') close to the Rhondda valley. The scenery on the way up the valley is functional as well as pleasant, since these forests not only clothe, in parts, industrial scars, but now moreover form the Afan Argoed Country Park.

Country Parks were instituted by the Countryside Act, 1969, as part of a policy for taking the question of the conflict between access and conservation, between recreation and natural scenery, more seriously. The White Paper suggested that country parks would enable people to enjoy themselves in the open air without travelling too far; they should, therefore, be located near to urban areas, in just the way that Afan Argoed is easily reached from Port Talbot. By this means, it was felt, the pressure on more remote and solitary places, and on the roads going to them, would be eased. The Act followed these recommendations and enabled Local Authorities, with the aid of 75 per cent grants, to set up such parks. Such things, of course, take time; but many authorities have been remarkably slow to set in motion this worthwhile process.

With the foresting of the mining hillsides, places such as Cymmer now find themselves suddenly in the middle of idyllic countryside. Not that they were ever, in location, anything other than rural. They were from the start small industrial colonies in the middle of wild mountains. If they now look like rural mountain villages, it is simply that the country around them has been the survivor, outlasting the industrial element, finally, in the sort of way the jungle does, creeping back in whenever pressure is eased. The small mining villages may yet find themselves welcoming tourists to their lovely scenery, their clean air and their peace and quiet; and if so, one of the things they will have to offer is a view of the odd, ironic inversions sometimes presented on the swings and roundabouts of the historical funfair.

XI RHYMNEY

While the areas of derelict land above Merthyr are, rather late in the day, being reclaimed, natural forces have done their own desultory reclamation elsewhere. The Rhymney valley consequently has a quasi-natural landscape, in which the turmoil to which the land has been subjected was in operation so long ago that it has come to seem not entirely a man-made turmoil.

Although here too new industry has been revitalizing the economic and social life, much of the Rhymney valley has not yet become redeveloped. As a result one can still see it, in places, as it originally was. The decaying terraces still give that jumbled, back-street, rag-and-bone atmosphere which so well accords with the image of old valley life.

The Rhymney valley actually continues all the way down to Caerphilly, though one thinks of it as ending, perhaps, at Ystrad Mynach. It has a lower branch uphill again to Senghenydd, a high and one-time isolated village typical of the smaller, mine-dominated places. Senghenydd experienced, in 1913, one of the worst of those recurring tragedies which have always beset the mining industry, when more than 400 of its miners died in a pit disaster. The village, like the terraces around Rhymney, still wears something of the down-trodden aspect of the coal age. And as one approaches Caerphilly, out of either of these valleys, it is very much a question, today, of passing from past to present.

Caerphilly is now a large place, a town surrounded by sprawling residential suburbs and industries. This development of Caerphilly, which was not very long ago a quiet and rather rural town, was an aspect of the massive effort to save industrial South Wales from the sort of cyclic depression and insecurity which had come to seem endemic. An industrial estate nearby bears the rather surprising name 'The Harold Wilson Industrial Estate'. No-one could accuse such a place of being over-romantic or poetic.

None of this, however, has resulted in the removal from its centre of its most enduring asset. Caerphilly Castle is said to be the second largest fortress in Europe (the largest being Windsor Castle) and it occupies a good 30 acres of the town's core, presenting an impressive and interesting example of a moated, concentric, thirteenth-century castle.

The present castle is the work of Gilbert de Clare, Lord of Glamorgan from 1266. There was, however, a Roman fort nearby which was possibly replaced by an early Welsh castle. Earl Gilbert's building, from 1268, of this large and strong fortress, was a symptom of his concern for the safety of the approaches to Cardiff in times of strong nationalistic movements in Wales. He had removed from power in the area Gruffydd ap Rhys, the hereditary ruler; but a more successful native prince was active in the north, and Llewelyn ap Gruffydd began to spread his rule southwards during the 1260s.

Gilbert's fears were not exaggerated. In 1268 Llewelyn arrived in Caerphilly, and destroyed the building which had only just been begun. De Clare persisted, and in 1271 he had started to build again. Llewelyn too evidently considered the matter to be important, and began to besiege the site works to prevent the castle's completion. Attempts by Henry III to settle the matter peacefully were overtaken by the impatience of de Clare and his fellow barons, who settled the matter by force. Llewelyn retreated and Caerphilly was finally built.

The castle, once completed, played only a sporadic and indeterminate part in history. It was occasionally useful to one side or the other in minor local revolts, and featured in Edward II's pitiful flight through Wales, in which he seems to have hurried rather wildly from one castle to another. It was only at the time of the Civil War, at a time when one would have expected castles to be going out of fashion, that it came back into use.

It is because of this that it now possesses its most famous feature. When Cromwell's army, following their normal precautionary policy, blew up as much as possible of what was left of the castle at the end of the war, they succeeded only, in the case of one tower, in shifting it out of vertical

Museum and City Hall, Civic Centre, Cardiff

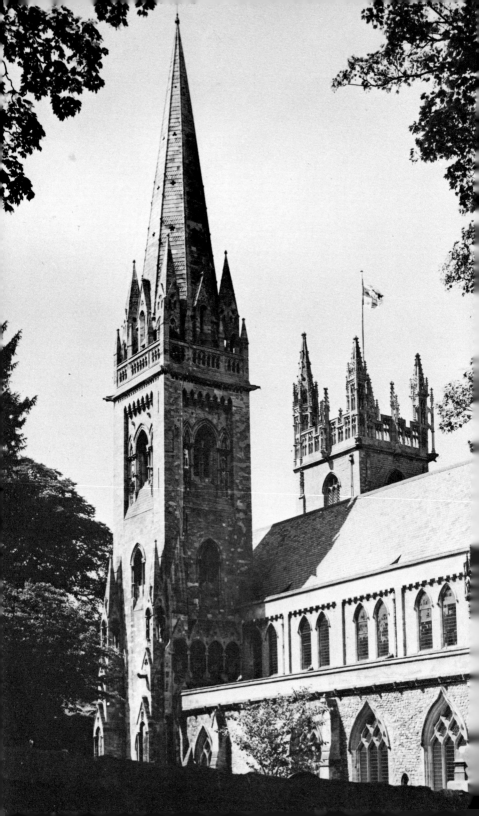

alignment. Though it cannot equal the Pisan campanile's
13-foot tilt, the leaning tower of Caerphilly, 9 feet out of the
vertical, is perhaps the most listing of all our listed buildings.

The castle as a whole conforms to an orthodox late-
thirteenth-century design. That is to say, it has a lightly-built
outer curtain surrounding an outer ward, inside which is the
real strength of the place in the form of a four-towered inner
curtain wall of considerable thickness enclosing, in the inner
ward, the buildings, such as the state rooms and the Hall,
where the life which it was constructed to defend took place.

Both curtain walls, inner and outer, have gateways,
intentionally set at slight angles to each other so that they
could not be rushed together. What makes Caerphilly so
large, and so impressive, is the fact that it did not stop at
these conventional, almost classic features. Its approaches
from the east are further protected by defensive works
beyond its surrounding moat, which themselves are again
separated from the outside world by another drawbridged
moat. And to the west again an insulating island called the
Hornwork, itself isolated from both land and castle by
drawbridges, had to be crossed before access to the outer
ward could be gained.

Caerphilly Castle is in fact itself an island in a lake, and this
appealing circumstance gives it its special nature. Its present
splendour owes much, in the way of swans and reflected
images, to the fact that its two moats still have water in
them. The water around the castle also forms an important
ingredient of its design, so that one can see, at Caerphilly, the
way in which the complementing factors of stone and water
have been used in combination to give an overall security.
The water part of the building was as planned and constructed as was the stone, being in fact a series of ditches, hollows
and embankments. It is our luck, and, one supposes, only
incidental to de Clare's intentions, that the whole effect is
beautiful.

The castle is in good repair, some of it in fact in a state
rather of restoration than survival, largely because of work
carried out by the Marquesses of Bute during the last century
and this. The castle passed into the hands of the Ministry of
Works, now the Department of the Environment, in 1949.

Llandaff Cathedral

The town of Caerphilly possesses, as if this were not enough, one other very large and notable construction. The opening of its hypermarket in the early 1970s caused some consternation, almost perhaps on the scale caused by the construction of its castle just seven hundred years before. It was then a form of commerce quite new to this country, and the dismay arose from its feared effects both on town-centre shopping and on the area's traffic. The principle is that everything the shopper requires is available in one single shop. The idea behind this thinking seems to be that it should be made as easy as possible to buy large quantities of goods. Certainly the size of the structure itself is intimidating, as indeed are some of the assumptions on which the concept is based. One of these is, evidently, that everybody owns a car.

In fact the idea of hypermarkets has not gone on to find the quick acceptance which was anticipated, either in South Wales or elsewhere, in the planning policies of the mid-70s. There has been much more a tendency towards the development of new town-centre shopping precincts, and the hypermarket at Caerphilly remains, at any rate for the time being, a rare, though not unique, example of what life in Britain might have been like.

Farmland intervenes, in the lower Sirhowy valley, at places such as Blackwood and Argoed, insulating the industrial belt at the bottom from the previously mining area near the valleys head. Tredegar, at the top of this valley, is, in character, like a large upland village. Grass slopes and plantations surround it, and its long, long terraces stretch like tentacles into the hills. It is not unlike a quiet, broad-streeted central Irish town, bland and unpretentious. For this reason, perhaps, its central feature, the town clock, stands out all the more startlingly.

It is a large iron monument surmounted by an ornate clock, and was erected in 1858. It commemorates the Duke of Wellington, but this, one feels, is little more than an excuse. The thing as a whole is magnificently pompous.

Up on the moorland, beside the road climbing out of Tredegar and near to the top of the Ebbw valley, stands a bulky and daunting memorial. It is a high, chilly spot, no

place to linger out of season, and there is something in the
bleakness, the austerity itself of the place that fits the
purpose of the monument. We do not bring messages of joy
and of freedom from care, still less blue skies, ideas of leisure
or amusement. We have an unavoidable reality to face, the
permanent division of interests of the economic classes and
the necessity of work as a prerequisite of survival in an
unsympathetic world. Four lumps of rough-cut stone on the
moorland say something disconcerting about the grandeur of
Cyfarthfa, or, to an even greater extent, the whimsicality of
such things as Castell Coch which is itself an accidental
memorial to the vast fortunes of the Butes.

The inscription on the largest, central block, says simply
that it was "here that Aneurin Bevan spoke to the people of
his constituency and of the world". The three lesser stones
surrounding it are marked "Tredegar", "Ebbw Vale" and
"Rhymney". The Bevan memorial as a whole has a simple
but resounding effect which could hardly be more appropriate. The large blocks of untrimmed stone sit categorically
on the hill, with all the forcefulness of an incontrovertible fact.

Ebbw Vale itself, with which the name of Bevan is perhaps
most easily associated, is now an important industrial town
with a busy shopping street. The long chain of monstrous
artefacts which goes to make up the Ebbw Vale steelworks
stretches down the valley below it.

In times of change (and are there, one starts to wonder,
any other sorts of times?) the present 25,000 inhabitants of
Ebbw Vale have felt again the dangers of being reliant on one
industry, however vast. British Steel's intentions for the
1970s involve a reduction of its labour force at Ebbw Vale.
Clearly if this is carried out alternative industries must be
found, since the population, as always in the South Wales
valleys, is greatly reluctant to leave. In the meantime
unemployment ominously threatens, in an area which was
just beginning to forget what large-scale unemployment was
like. It is, all too clearly, a recurrent pattern.

The population of Ebbw Vale fell from over 30,000 in the
late 1920s, when the depression caught it at its height. The
1930s, which saw, in valleys such as this and the Rhondda,
unemployment levels of 40 to 50 per cent, were the most

dramatic, and seem most immediate to current generations, of the many periods of recession which the valleys have suffered. Between 1921 and 1939, 400,000 people moved out of industrial South Wales. In the Rhymney valley in 1932 46 per cent of the insurable male population were unemployed. In Pontypridd in the same year the figure reached a peak of 76 per cent. Ironically the new steelworks at Ebbw Vale (the reduction of which now threatens hardship in the '70s) was introduced, on Government initiative, in the 1930s, to cope with the closure of the mines and ironworks.

Keir Hardie had anticipated, by his success at Merthyr, the rise of the labour movement which was to accompany the economic and social difficulties which the area had brought upon itself. By 1929 the Labour Party had increased to 25 members in Wales, most of whom were in the urban south.

Just below the town and works of Ebbw Vale the village of Cwm, as much as anywhere, provides a classic example of a Valleys town, being all regular terraces and black-soiled slopes above them. The effect of this linear planning is clear: you are never more than a few paces from the open hillside. Abertillery, in the next valley, the Ebbw Fach, is slightly less consistent, being all built on one slope of the valley. But because of this the stacked rows of old cottages, each with its chimney and fire-smoke, each with the regular outlined windows, present, from across the valley, a striking display of this strict architectural form.

South Welsh mining-town terraces. As distinctive and forceful a form as Swiss chalets, Georgian manors, or Byzantine churches. Almost all the settlements were erected between 1860 and 1910, and the houses consequently are of a fairly regular plan. They often have three upstairs bedrooms, though some only possess two, and three downstairs rooms in all. When they were built they lacked any normal sanitation, and it was common for one lavatory, outside, to be shared between five or six houses. In 1911, by which time most of the urbanization had taken place, there was an average of 5.6 persons per house in the urban districts of the Cardiff hinterland. For every new house erected between 1901 and 1911 there were, such was the increase in the population of the area, 7.5 people waiting to occupy it.

The old terraces have not, now, entirely disappeared, because it has proved cheaper in many cases to modernize old houses (which are also cheap to buy) than to build or buy a new one. Travel-to-work has become a normal practice, and people regard this as an acceptable price to pay not only for the cheaper housing but for the social atmosphere, which they find pleasanter in the villages than in the new estates.

Now the window-surrounds are brightly painted, and, at the back, the complementing row of cars outside the doors tells of the present tolerable conditions. The cottages may well, when they were built, have played their part in instituting what might have been, in effect, a sort of serfdom. They have survived into a different sort of epoch, and in places like Abertillery have managed to adapt themselves to this and to continue to function.

Large ungrassed tips still dominate the upland scenery above Blaenavon, south of Brynmawr, where small rows of cottages sit with a certain hopelessness confronting the bleak scenery. But reclamation is creeping up towards them, and in time even these will be merged with the landscape. One gets the feeling that we are now, in many places, saying a last goodbye to the coal industry.

Just how many pits are still open it would be hard, or rash, to say. The industry is as subject as ever to sudden fluctuations. It is neither inconceivable that old mines may be reopened nor that the very last one may finally close. The targets of the nationalized industry were reduced in 1956 and again in 1965. The industry contracted rapidly after 1960. Enormous quantities of coal still remain, for instance in the western anthracite valleys such as the Dulais, north of Neath. But hardly any collieries, even there, continue to mine it. There are no collieries left in the Heads of the Valleys area; most which are left, moderate-sized units, are on the Monmouthshire side of the belt. One can, at least, make positive statements about the past. There were in all 25 collieries still at work in 1970. Of these only one was in the Rhondda Fawr, and only nine in the anthracite fields of the west.

One of the difficulties with preserving the remnants of the industry, has, rather surprisingly, been the problem of recruiting labour. In 1973 (when it was said that 600 men per week were leaving the mining industry in Britain, and up to perhaps a hundred per week in South Wales), the South Wales pits were over 1,600 men short, and spent the sum of £60,000 in advertising on television and cinema screens for labour. The man-power has, of course, been absorbed by the vast new industries, where pay and conditions are more attractive to the new age group. Miners bitterly complain of the false set of values which rewards the production of coal so poorly in proportion to the difficulties of the job and the value of the product to the nation. The labour shortage in the meantime led to uneconomic production, and to a situation in which the coalfields had become a million tons below its target.

Conditions are part, but not all, of the causes of the withdrawal from the industry. Much of the trouble is a social one, and is not improved by changes taking place within the technology of coal-mining. The policy of closing mines which are running uneconomically in the hopes of providing a full work-force for another mine nearby has not always worked. Loyalty to a certain mine is a factor which keeps the remnant of the miners at work. As conditions are improved by the introduction of mechanization at the coal-face, in place of the pick-and-shovel business of the last generation, one would expect people to be readier to take the job; the reverse, however, often seems to be the case. It is still unpleasant, working below ground, and in cold, cramped, dirty and dangerous circumstances, and now one is being controlled by the pace of a machine rather than doing a job to which one could bring the qualities of skill and endeavour. One of the things which for a time kept men working in mines was the sense of comradeship built up by the old system of team-work. With the increase in the use of machinery this becomes impossible. One has no contact with other workers, and in any case the noise makes talk impossible. The pressure of keeping up with the machine combines with the lack of any sense of achievement to make the work monotonous and unsatisfying. Improvement of conditions then, is not, apparently, the answer. If one is going to be on production-line work it might as well be above ground, in greater comfort and for higher pay.

The answer for mining is, quite possibly, an even greater degree of automation. The process of winning coal can, in theory, be completely automated and operated remotely. One day, perhaps, white coats will replace black faces. Some degree of this is likely in the near future, if the industry can survive its present troubles of the transition period, in which men and machinery continue to struggle for dominance.

The modern boom in the South Wales economy has, in the meantime, been in the field of the manufacturing industries, such as the large Hoover factory below Merthyr, and the vehicle businesses of Cardiff, Llanelli and Swansea. The latest phase in fact started with the Second World War, when key industries of the national economy were dispersed westwards, and supplemented there by the wartime ordnance factories. After the war the ordnance factories were converted, the government provided regional development aid, one hundred and twelve government-sponsored factories were formed, and unemployment fell from 20 per cent to 2.8 per cent in ten years. The high demand for coal and steel continued into the late '50s, but the 1960s saw the change to manufacturing industries. The motor industry in particular expanded into South Wales at this time. By the early 1970s the unemployment figure seldom exceeded four per cent. The post-war boom, however, was by then running out; and in the familiar manner of South Wales economic life it started to swing back.

One would not on the whole suspect the possibility, however, of another large-scale regional depression. The place seems far too highly developed and active for that, and now, at any rate, everybody is conscious of the dangers. So much large industry rings the main centres of population that it would be hard to check its confident progression.

Pontypool is such a place. Not somewhere of special charm, but simply a South Wales industrial town. It provides, in addition to the large industries on its outskirts, a shopping and commercial centre for the eastern valleys. Large and amorphous, and normally surrounded by hectic traffic, what it does best, perhaps, is offer for comparison a specimen of the planning of the past to set against the futuristic present of Cwmbran.

Cwmbran, just south of Pontypool, is one of Britain's new towns. It began its development during the 1960s, but towns take time to develop and mature and it still looks, and feels, almost uncomfortably new. If it has not yet grown a spirit of its own, there is no real reason to suppose that this will not eventually arise. Many towns have been new once, and Cwmbran stands a better chance of becoming likeable than most of them ever did.

It is a large shopping precinct surrounded by ample free car-parking, with office blocks rising over it and a great deal of adjacent low-rise housing. It is the latter which seems the most promising, being built on a human scale; not beautiful, but planned in a traditional style, and, unlike so much modern housing, not such that it imposes itself on the people who have to live in it. Perhaps it is even uninspired, but if so one tends to say "thank goodness". Other new developments such as Butetown in Cardiff have been uninspired as well, of course, but here in Cwmbran the lie of the land combines with the planning of the layout to give variety to the views of the streets, so that the rows of houses acquire individuality and avoid that overall impression of standardization.

At least Cwmbran in general gives the appearance of having been made for people rather than fellow-architects, and its emerging character seems to be that of a place which is pleasant, spacious, and undemanding. If that sort of thing represents the future of South Wales, it is certainly no worse than the past.

PART FIVE

THE CAPITAL

XII THE VALE OF GLAMORGAN

It is not, in any strict sense, a vale; not, that is, something the sides of which slope down to a recognizable central line. In fact it is not a clearly-defined unit at all. It happens that the bulge of South Wales which obtrudes into the Bristol Channel between Porthcawl and Cardiff is all green lowland country. That, roughly, is the Vale of Glamorgan. The A48 bisects it; hills rising to the mining districts bound it on the north; its south side is a curve of coastal country on the Bristol Channel.

The Vale went through that same pattern of history which applied to most of southern South Wales. That is, it was occupied by Norman barons shortly after the Conquest, had imposed upon it the Norman feudal system, and became, as a result, a settled and prosperous country dotted with castles and great manor houses; and occupied, on the one hand, by rich and powerful families, and on the other by villages of well-established country people living within limited horizons. Scenery is social as well as geological, and there is no doubt that the pattern of land-owning and life style which the Normans imposed on the area accounts for much of the sedate and imperturbable loveliness of the countryside today.

Bridgend is the Vale's largest town, a considerable shopping centre with a business-like, purposeful character. In its nature it is, as it happens, far from being characteristic of the Vale of Glamorgan, in which it finds itself geographically, and in fact many people would instinctively exclude it from the area. Its orientation is on the one hand towards the coalfields of the Ogmore valley, and on the other towards the vast industrial estate with which its innate prosperity is supplemented. This, extended by 200 acres in 1967 and

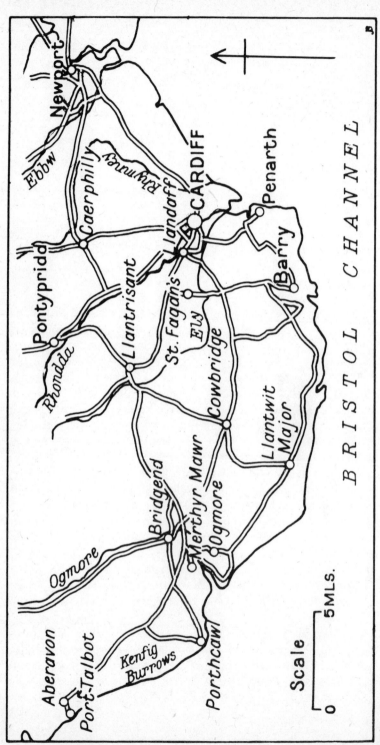

BRISTOL CHANNEL

Scale

5 MLS.

0

The Capital

already large, was a fortunate development from the war-time ordnance factory. This was, at that time, Britain's largest ammunition-filling factory, at its peak employed 36,000 people, most of them women, and its presence at Bridgend led to a climate of social attitudes ready adapted to post-war, female-labour-oriented factory work.

Thus Bridgend is far from typical of an area which is overwhelmingly agricultural and traditional. One only has to go a little way off the A48, however, and into the country lanes, to experience these qualities to the full. Ewenny, for instance, less than a mile from Bridgend, is as soaked in tranquility as a place can reasonably be expected to be.

In many ways it is surprising, but fortunate, that Ewenny is not better known. The old mill sells antiques, and up a lane nearby, almost unsignposted and difficult to find, is Ewenny Priory, a perfect Norman building. It is hidden away and quite untrumpeted, and one could quite easily never know that it was there. Perhaps a part, at least, of its great charm lies in this diffidence. Once there, even, one might quite easily miss the best piece of it – which is not the nave, partitioned off and still in use as the Parish Church, but the chancel, at the eastern side of the partition, which is entered through another door. This small, bare room, a cave-like, squatly-rounded Norman interior, has about it a sombre ancientness, an awe-inducing effect out of all proportion to its size. Durham Cathedral towers and looms with the same result; Ewenny's chancel does it quietly and in miniature, and quite without resorting to drama or grandeur. It impresses by its purity of style and its lack of affectation.

The Priory was founded in 1141, and, as can easily be seen, the major part of it was fortified. The bulk of the buildings now are in the care of the Department of the Environment.

From Ewenny, with a good map, one could find one's way down the maze of small lanes wandering around Merthyr Mawr, some of which lead down into the valley itself. It is only a small collection of cottages, secluded by substantial trees, on a road going to nowhere. But its little valley forms as calm and pastoral a part of the world as any place in Britain. Merthyr Mawr warren, beyond the village, is famous for having produced archaeological finds from the Stone and Bronze Ages. It is a large-scale sand-dune area running all the way down to the sea and along this stretch of coast — as far, in fact, as the outskirts of Porthcawl. Blown sand has accumulated into ridges, marram grass establishing itself, stabilizing the sand and hence catching further blowing sand, until the dunes (some of them, at 200 feet high, fully-qualified hills) have completely covered the land where, it seems, dense populations of ancient civilizations once lived.

Of this central, inland part of the Vale, the main town and social focus is undoubtedly Cowbridge, which, unlike Bridgend, is a true part of the Vale in all respects. It is an almost completely linear place, with countryside at all its back doors. Though a major town in an otherwise rural area, it typifies the Vale's predominantly somnolent manner by dozing quietly, continually, with normally a drowsy mutter coming from its many old dark-roomed, beer-smelling pubs.

Pubs in fact, and all they stand for, play a big part in the area's healthy agricultural life, and little clusters of them tend to crop up in the countryside, with sometimes a small village attached, as if by way of an excuse.

Though it is rather difficult to see how, (so long and thin is it now), Cowbridge was once walled, and fragments of this wall — including one of the original three gates — remain. The town, which may originally have been the site of a Roman camp, became an important market town during the thirteenth century. A plaque commemorates an eighteen-century resident of the district, (though not actually of the town itself), a stone-mason's son by the name of Edward Williams, who became well-known in Wales under his bardic name of Iolo Morgannwg.

The revival of old Welsh literature, which had its culmination in the publication, in 1846, of Lady Charlotte Guest's translation of the *Mabinogion*, owes a great deal to the scholarship and enthusiasm of Iolo Morgannwg. So too, unfortunately, does the over-romanticized image of bardic and druidic goings-on which has served to mislead people as to the true nature of Celtic culture and tradition. Iolo and his revival rose to prominence during the 1790s; the movement was chiefly centred on a small group of expatriate Welshmen in London, of whom Iolo was a leader. It was the end of a period during which their national culture had fallen into neglect; the medieval manuscripts in which the chiefly poetic literary tradition of pre-anglicized Wales was preserved were scattered in various collections, and in some cases unrecognized even by their owners. The discovery and transcription of these, from which resulted the realization that Wales had a rich and substantial ancient literature, was mainly the work of Iolo. Unfortunately both for his reputation and for Welsh tradition, he also did two greatly less scholarly things. He included among the genuine transcriptions a great deal of expert and painstaking forgery, so that it is only recently that anyone has been able to decide, with certainty, what was the product of the early Middle Ages and what that of Morgannwg's convincing imagination. His second lapse of integrity was the invention of the Gorsedd.

'The Gorsedd of Bards of the Isle of Britain' is an assembly of prominent Welshmen which performs the ceremonial aspects of the annual National Eisteddfod. These rituals, semi-mystical, semi-Christian, and encumbered with regalia, stone circles and religious robes, punctuate the Eisteddfod programme at its significant points. They are presided over by an Archdruid, under whom a hierarchy of officials, druids, and bards forms the complete body. There is no reason at all to suppose that any component of all this is in any way connected with the druids (priestly teachers in Celtic Europe during Roman times) or the druid religion, nor indeed with any early Welsh assemblies. Iola Morgannwg invented it all.

This invention took place largely in London and during the year 1792. He and his group of London Welshmen held the first Gorsedd meeting, in the summer of that year, on Primrose Hill. Meanwhile the Eisteddfod, a competitive musical and literary gathering (an institution which had always existed in one form or another in Wales) was, at the time, gaining in popularity. Several successful ones had taken place in North Wales, and when, during the first decade of the next century, with the great new interest in Welsh culture for which Iolo had been partly responsible, the habit gained ground in the south, he managed, by persuasion, to have his new ceremonial system grafted into the Eisteddfod tradition.

There it has somehow stayed, and today remains unshakably welded into the fabric of the annual National Eisteddfod, in spite of the factors militating against it. That is in spite of our knowledge of its lack of authenticity and in spite of the inherent foolishness of the idea of a number of respectable middle-aged Welshmen wearing nighties in public and chanting bogus rites.

Edward Williams, Iolo Morgannwg, died and was buried (in 1826) at Flemingston, where he had lived since 1795, and a memorial in the village church there, three miles south-east of Cowbridge, commemorates him.

The mainly low-level rolling country around Cowbridge is bordered by a line of hills, through which the Ely valley comes down out of the coalfield. On the ridge of one of these is the town of Llantrisant. The old village, topped by its church, looks down over the Vale, and marks its northern boundary. Below it the modern town spreads down the hill, a place now reprieved of its one-time fate of being the focus of a new area of population. The introduction of the Royal Mint, as part of a policy of national decentralization, was to have been only a preliminary step in a trend which, by the end of the century, threatened (or promised) Llantrisant with a possible population of 130,000. It was objected that the new town would draw still more people from the dying valley villages, and further add to their social and economic difficulties. Faced with strong local opposition, the Welsh Office wisely withdrew the plan, leaving the new part of Llantrisant to develop slowly on its own. Down the other side, over the ridge, the view of the Ely Valley opens, and just below the perched village ponies and cattle graze among the picnickers on Llantrisant Common. The name of the town denotes that its church is dedicated to three saints, one of whom, predictably, is Illtyd.

The eastern end of the Vale, where the rivers Taff and Ely run on roughly parallel courses towards the Severn, becomes the outskirts of Cardiff; and places such as Llandaff and St Fagan's belong more to the capital than to its hinterland, and so will be dealt with later. Cardiff also extends its influence, in a way, to Penarth, which, however, as a respectable resort in its own right, has a claim to be treated separately. It also exemplifies a rather surprising feature of the Vale of Glamorgan; in contrast to its tranquil rustic interior, the coastline, which is every bit as much a part of the Vale, has more than its natural share of holiday resorts.

As it happens Penarth is not, by nature, ideally suited to this role of seaside place. It is the ridge of an escarpmented headland, steep-sloped and with difficult access to the beach. It fulfils better its other role of pleasant residential satellite to Cardiff. The town and Esplanade have a leisurely atmosphere, but fail to compensate for the slightly uncomfortable impression given by their physical nature. The cold-looking mud-coloured water is far down below the pier, flanked by a stony beach.

A very different sort of thing in almost all respects is Barry, only a short way along the coast, past Sully with its island and ancient church. Barry is largely in a different world from either the Vale's inland acres or Penarth's sedate suburban blandness.

The town of Barry itself is actually large and urban, having been brought quite suddenly into existence on the completion of its dockyard, as a rival to Cardiff, in 1889. The population of Barry was, in 1881, only 85. Ten years later it was over 13,000. Now it is 42,000, and still flourishing. The docks were, it seems, a success. In 1911 Barry shipped out eleven million tons of coal, and in 1913 it superseded Cardiff as the largest coal-exporting port in the world.

Giraldus Cambrensis, whose family name was de Barri, had, with good reason, a special interest in the place. His father was a Norman lord who had acquired South Wales estates, and taken his name from Barry Island, which was one of his possessions. Giraldus, without undue modesty, says this himself.

From hence a noble family, of the maritime parts of South Wales, who owned this island and the adjoining estates, received the name of de Barri.

Then it was an island, and so described both by Giraldus and by Leland; but subsequently the docks have connected it to the mainland, and it now appears – what one can see of it – as simply a raised headland on a complicated piece of coast. It is, however, largely invisible beneath the vast concoctions which go to make up Butlin's Camp.

Barry the holiday place, as distinct from the port and town, is divided into two main sections, Barry Island and the Knap. The Knap provides the gentler type of recreation, extending to ballroom dancing, and a steep and stony beach which is supplemented by the swimming-pool at Knap Lido. It is on Barry Island itself that all the fun happens. It happens at Whitmore Bay.

Whitmore Bay: long, broad stretch of crisp sand under one's toes. Beach-balls and Coke cans and female children screaming in the always icy water of the tide. What is it about these long afternoons of August, sunny and salty, that has entrenched them in the national notion of happiness? The connection with childhood, presumably, which, for many people, is, at any rate in its edited form, seaside holidays all the way. They can go back down to Barry and re-enter it.

Over the sandy beach, however, rears a constricting, excluding element. Butlins have cordoned off a complete headland, with a rigorousness and an aspect of menace worthy of the Ministry of Defence. Their tiers and tiers of living quarters overlooking the bay present, visually, possibly one of the ugliest structures ever devised. The Camp moreover provides the bulk of the holiday accommodation in the resort, and so the remaining liveliness of the seafront tends to go dead at night. Day visitors account for a good part of the crowds, other than camp residents, populating the beach. Even at the height of the season the seafront tends to fall, at night, into a waste of scattered chip-papers and closed shops. The kids sink into the cellar-bars and discos, as they do everywhere, but Mum and Dad and the push-chair, and Irene and little David, and William, the mongrel, have all gone home.

One thing remains alive, however, and that is the gigantic funfair, which is fiercely exuberant and adept at its business. Tradition and innovation blend, not without some self-conscious posing, as in the case of the ornate roundabout which claims, in splendid lettering, to be "patronized and enjoyed by all classes". Though this is hardly true, and

Monnow Bridge, Monmouth

though the carved wooden horses have sadly been replaced by plastic ones, at least the convention remains the same, and it spreads the smell of fun thickly in the air. The Good Life takes many forms, and candy-floss is one of them. Pop-music and the whirling lights, and the whole atmosphere made up of sticks of rock, bawdy postcards and the onion-frying smell of hot-dog stands. One may or may not like it, but there is no denying that it is one of the few things that the British do with flare.

Barry Island has, by contrast with its holiday camp and funfair, some slight elements of more restrained enjoyment, in the form of a yacht harbour and a small secluded cove, Jackson's Bay, enclosed under its sandstone cliffs. Barry sits, in any case, on the edge of a strip of level country which is pleasant and rural. And the coastline reverts to this gentler nature as soon as one is through the town.

Rhoose Airport, South Wales's major civil airport, lies between Barry and Llantwit Major, but does not greatly obtrude into the life of the area. The large jets now and then scream away over the sea. Neither this nor any other aspect of reality upsets the pace of life of Llantwit.

In spite of its memorable and resounding name, the village of Llantwit Major is uncompromisingly villagey. People sit talking in the space in its centre which can hardly be called a square, and its single winding street seems to be composed entirely of small old houses. It is the church itself which is Major, a grand but unpretentious building with a tall, white, ancient nave. It has, inside, a dramatically imposing air which owes a lot to the rising levels, from west to east, which lead one up towards the altar.

The earliest Christian foundations were made of wood, and such would of course be the form of that founded here by Illtyd in the very early years of the sixth century. Illtyd's biography was written some centuries later, but a very early document, the "Life of St Samson", (which, coming as it does from the early part of the seventh century, belongs almost to the time of living-memory of Illtyd's lifetime), refers to him and to the monastery of Llan Illtyd Fawr. The "Life of St Samson" portrays Illtyd as being a man of great learning, and even credits him with powers of divination.

Agincourt Square, Monmouth

"Were I to begin to relate all his wondrous works I should be led to excess." Hagiography frequently finds itself in just such a state, but there is no doubt, from this and other records, of Illtyd's enormous status in early Christian times. The monastery at Llan Illtyd became, under his rule, a teaching college. Many of the 'saints' of sixth-century Wales emerged from there, including Samson, whose biography consequently gives us details of the college at Llantwit (as the name eventually became). It was said that Illtyd's pupils moreover included, besides the clergy, members of the ruling classes; Maelgwyn Gwynedd, who was to become a powerful, though unstable, king of the whole of North Wales, came there for his education. One of the most famous pupils was, reputedly, the historian Gildas, an emigrant from the north of Britain whose diatribe against the state of his time gives us a strong, if partisan, view of sixth-century Britain and its rulers.

If indeed these leaders of the time did attend St Illtyd's college, then his teaching would have had considerable impact on his period. One direct result was undoubtedly the massive spread of Christianity which issued from the evangelists educated at Llan Illtyd.

The Middle Ages brought the arrival of the Normans and the loss of Celtic independence. The Renaissance brought the Dissolution, and the end of monastic life. All we are left now of the long periods during which the site was occupied by a large and active religious community, is this church.

The Church of St Illtyd as it is at present dates from the twelfth, thirteenth, fourteenth, and fifteenth centuries. It is in two distinct halves, one older in origin and narrower than the other. The western of these two occupies the site of the Norman church, which probably, in turn, replaced Illtyd's original building. It was, however, rebuilt in the fifteenth century, and so is actually, as a structure, younger than the eastern half which was added to it. Only the doorway of the old Norman church, built perhaps as early as 1100, remains.

The eastern part of the whole, today the nave and chancel of the present functioning church, was built, as an extension to the old church, in the late thirteenth century. The tower which divides the two was added to the earlier church in

about 1200, at the time rising over the crossing of the
transepts and chancel, the site of which was occupied by the
new church.

St Illtyd's has two special claims to attention. One is the
magnificent collection of ancient stones in the western
church. The other is the murals, uncovered during the 1950s,
which decorate the walls of the eastern church.

Several among the stones exemplify the fine Celtic
decorations built-up of ingenious and elaborate inter-woven
lines and curves. Some of them are memorials to local leaders
for whom the Abbey formed a respectable burial place; their
dates are reliably thought to be mostly of the ninth century.
Together they form a fine collection of skilful and imaginative stonework.

The murals also have this quality of displaying for us the
care and craftsmanship of an age. In spite of their partly
decayed condition they still glow with a spirit of enthusiasm
which has transformed itself naturally into warm and rich
colours. Although they cover a fairly long period, they
possess a basic similarity of style, a directness and clarity
which is clearly aimed at communication. The earliest are
dated (by deduction, only) at 1300. The latest of those now
visible is clearly the one which, in 1604, celebrates the
accession of King James I, depicting his coat of arms. The
murals survive despite the efforts of the Puritans, whose
reaction against what must then have been a highly-coloured,
perhaps even gaudy, interior, is not entirely incomprehensible. They scraped off what they could of the paint, and
covered the whole thing with whitewash.

A little way along the coast from Llantwit is St Donat's
Castle, an old Norman seat which, in 1925, was acquired by
William Randolph Hearst, the prototype American millionaire,
who thus, presumably, fulfilled the ambition of all American
fantasists: to own a genooine old European castle.

St Donat's had been in existence since approximately
1300, and had been occupied by the same family until the
eighteenth century. Hearst was born in 1863, and took over
his father's paper, the *San Francisco Examiner*, at the age of
24. His Kane-like progress then took place within the next
ten years. He resorted to methods then either unheard-of or

considered unthinkable, such as the banner headline and the use of sensational material. And whatever the morality of the methods the practical point was proved, since he trebled the circulation of the *New York Journal* in a single year. He then bought up most of the other American newspapers, and is said to have multiplied his initial multi-million-dollar fortune by ten. By 1914 he had become involved in the movie business, and when, in 1925, he came to St Donat's, his guests there included (much, no doubt, to the excitement of the locals of the time) people like Marion Davies.

Citizen Hearst approached the question of the improvement of St Donat's with a certain amount of Disneyland extravagance, which included the removal and re-erection of the roof and other parts of a fourteenth-century Priory, formerly at Bradenstoke in Wiltshire. The impressive setting which results, with its formal gardens and outdoor heated swimming-pool, is now the home of Atlantic College. This, strictly The United World College of the Atlantic, is an international sixth-form school, founded in 1962.

Atlantic College was the first of an intended international network of such colleges, providing pre-university courses for 16 and 17 year-olds. The emphasis is on international understanding and the interdependence of nations. Students are normally sent, to complete their last two years of school, on scholarships raised in their home countries. They come from many different cultures in all parts of the world, study for an international matriculation exam, and disperse again to more than 150 universities in more than twenty countries.

St Donat's, as a village, and Marcross nearby, are definitely farming places. Friesians abound in the fields, and the smell of cow-sheds blows through their streets. At this point a lane goes down towards the coast, and anyone who wonders what the softly rolling land is made of should go on down it to Nash Point, where a section is cut through the Vale of Glamorgan where it ends in the sea, as if for educational demonstration purposes (this is what is meant by 'strata'). The cliffs all around rise in horizontal sections, and even the beach is made of the same flat pieces; the sea comes in over layered pavements. One result of this remarkable piece of geology is that the Nash Point area is not one of sandy beaches. A little further along the coast, however, at Southerdown, there is a magnificent stretch of sand.

Though the Vale of Glamorgan is agricultural, it is also seaside. This unusual combination can be seen in areas such as the slopes around Ogmore-by-Sea, where the arable land comes right down to the shore. Beyond, the bay where the Ogmore river emerges sweeps round towards Porthcawl, its arc encircling the dark line of the Tusker Rock. This, although formidable and notorious, lacks the almost mythical status of its black and towering namesake off the coast of Wexford. The area of Ogmore is bland and sandy (pony-rides on the spacious beaches, and picnics on the sandhills), but the swimming, owing to currents at the mouth of the Ogmore river, is, in places, dangerous.

There are, no doubt, many who would prefer to think of Porthcawl as not being, at all, in that largely idyllic and reposeful area known as the Vale of Glamorgan. Kenfig, Pyle, Laleston, Merthyr Mawr and Ogmore, yes . . . Porthcawl, however, lies in the middle of them and cannot be willed away.

Why should we think in this way about it, rather than with pride? There is a case for claiming that it is in fact the best thing of its kind. The conclusion almost follows inevitably from the fact that it is inconceivable that anything could better fulfil the particular requirements. One might suppose at first that something which surpasses everything else in its class has a sort of natural right to excellence. That this is, in practice, not so, is due to our habit of judging things by our standards rather than their own. If things were judged according to the success with which they achieve their own aims, then we should have no difficulty with Porthcawl.

Three thousand caravans support its flank. Three thousand caravans is a lot of caravans, possibly one of the largest collections brought together in any one uninterrupted group anywhere in Europe. Porthcawl itself, whether it likes it or not, is a town tacked onto the end of this, an abutment to this long, consistent caravan city. As a town it is not either negligible or distinguished. It is a modest and adequate seaside resort. It has one or two sound, traditional hotels, and the usual collection of cafés, shops, and small unambitious pubs. None of that is specially significant, contiguous to the Coney Beach Pleasure Park and the ocean of caravans beyond it.

Comparison with Barry would suggest itself, even if the places were not so close as to fall within the same county, area, and chapter. On the surface the comparison is quantitative: Porthcawl seems larger. The rowdiness of the funfair is louder, the pubs around it fuller, the beach both wider and more closely-packed with bodies. Both have their self-contained areas of accommodation (Butlin's in one case, the caravans in the other) so that their true extent is partly hidden from the town. These impressions of size, however, are not the only distinguishing features. There is, in fact, a qualitative comparison to be made. Though it is hard to believe it possible, Porthcawl is even more lacking in sophistication, even more forceful in its all-out garishness, than Barry.

The caravans form a complete constructed world. They stretch for miles and miles along the shore beyond the funfair, and among them are spread shops, amusements, cinemas, bars, swimming pools, and even a church. This unexpected facility, however, makes an accidental but appropriate point. It is small and insignificant, and over it towers a massive bingo hall. The latter, huge and self-confident, has the awe-inspiring splendour which the humble church behind it lacks. Here is the real cathedral of the diocese of Porthcawl, and its congregation queues at the west door in the early evening.

In its way this holiday complex is both extreme and superb. Presumably there is, somewhere in America, a funland larger and louder, but it would lack the strong Welsh accent which here, somehow, succeeds in relating everything to humanity, to the small-town standards of reference of real life. If all this falls short of perfection, by its own terms, this is due to the constricting influence of the British licensing laws, which treat us still as if we were all at school. Such things should, correctly, go on all night.

North, again, sand has blown over the land, burying completely the old borough of Kenfig (though somehow leaving Kenfig pool, an extremely large sheet of natural fresh water), and piling up for miles where Kenfig Burrows go on and on to become Margam Burrows. The dunes are rich in flora; orchids and other unusual flowers flourish among them. Pressure now from the north and east is cutting into them and reducing their considerable extent. Already about 1,200 acres of sand have given way to the encroachment of development. The wasteland is becoming populated again.

XIII CARDIFF

Cardiff is on the river Taff, one mile from the Bristol Channel. It was a Roman stronghold during the third century A.D., and the Roman fort became a Norman castle during the eleventh. The town received its charter in 1147, was visited by Henry II, is mentioned by Giraldus, and had become by then the capital of the Lordship of Glamorgan. This in turn became the County of Glamorgan after the Act of Union in 1536, and Cardiff moved into the role of county town. Its population remained at under two thousand until the start of the eighteenth century, but from 1794 onwards it started to grow. That was the time of the opening of the Glamorgan-shire canal, which ran from Cardiff up to Merthyr. By 1861 the population of Cardiff and Llandaff was nearly 33,000.

The natural result of the canal and the rise in the trade of coal was the building of the docks. Docks were built in 1839 and 1854, and by 1871 the population had risen to 56,911. Cardiff became, in that year, the largest town in Wales, overtaking Merthyr where the population was then only 54,741. More docks were built in 1887, and the population jumped again. In 1891 it had reached 128,915. In 1905 Cardiff became officially a city, and the export of coal reached a peak in 1912. It became the official capital of Wales only as late as December 1955, not without dissent from north and central Wales. Today the population is in the 270,000s, and, though the city itself may not be greatly affected, the area of Cardiff and Newport (between and behind which lie large areas of new housing) has in general

recently been experiencing an increase in population due to
inward migration, over and above its natural increase.

Perhaps it takes a bit of time for a capital city to get
settled in. Edinburgh and Dublin have a strength of character
which Cardiff, as a whole, lacks. The one in its austerity, the
other in its mellowness, they impose their atmospheres of
national and metropolitan identity with unmistakable firm-
ness. A lot of it is of course due to architectural consistency,
and Edinburgh without its tall, iron-grey houses, or Dublin
without those lovely Georgian proportions would lack,
undoubtedly, the strong auras which they display. But
Cardiff, in comparison, lacks a quality less tangible; it lacks
the ability to get one emotionally involved. Edinburgh for all
its drizzle is lovable for itself, and Dublin evokes in every
square or corner a special tide of nostalgia. It is hard to
imagine anyone leaning over the parapet of Cardiff Bridge
and getting the same heavy wave of sense of place (with all its
cargo of city-consciousness and national identity) that is so
hard to avoid when, from O'Connell Bridge, one watches the
thick and slow surface of the Liffey moving past the Quays.

Fairer, perhaps, would be comparison with Liverpool,
since Cardiff is essentially a port and provincial town. And in
fact echoes of Liverpool abound, not only because of the
admixture in the populations of both cities of Irish and Welsh
elements. Some patches of architecture which have not yet
been torn down indicate a former wealth and splendour,
memorials to the great trading days of both cities. At the
back of it is the knowledge of the docks, and the sub-world
which goes with them, clinging, outside the city centre, to
doomed buildings and areas which are gradually, painfully,
being edged into extinction. Liverpool as a port has greater
grandeur and more force of personality, as has, if it comes to
that, many a port to greater degrees still. Naples, Casablanca,
Barcelona. What has Bute Street got with which to challenge
the Barrio Chino?

They reply, of course, that it is not what it once was.
Patently it is not, nor even what it will shortly be. As the
cranes move inwards the remaining area of the old streets of
the city centre takes on increasingly the run-down air which
preceeds redevelopment: the inevitable air of hopelessness

which a building wears under the shadow of its gleaming new glass-and-concrete neighbours. Perhaps there is at least this sort of excuse for these sad transitional streets, but one suspects that to be excused is more than they deserve. Architecturally much of Cardiff was never very good. The overall lack of character of the shopping streets is only partially relieved by the arcades, which consequently stand out as being of special interest. Elsewhere they would be a minor feature.

Soon, anyway, it will all be over. Standardized blocks gradually replace the unexceptional city streets. Will we come to love the new city, we wonder (looking upwards), more than we loved the old? The new towers – often here, for some reason, in dark materials which simulate, or anticipate, the application of grime – seem mainly to have been imposed with little consideration for aesthetic values. Where there is no over-riding question of taste, but instead one of expediency, the result is a lack of individuality. There is little variation possible in the most efficient use of glass and concrete, and even when there is it is sometimes easier to use a standard design. We are left with indistinguishable townscapes: London, Frankfurt, Liverpool, Rotterdam, Dusseldorf, Cardiff. We no longer know where we are.

The trend is sad, because Cardiff had in many ways a better chance than most cities. It had, at one time, a strong inbuilt character. It had a spacious layout of the city centre, which clearly asks for nothing but a civilized treatment of the streets around it. It had, in any case, the opportunity to give expression to the natural self-importance of a nation.

Much of the space in the city centre is occupied by those twin monuments, both in their way grandiose and superb: Cardiff Castle and Cardiff Arms Park. They compete with each other for importance, on either side of Castle Street. The Taff wanders past them both like a country river. With such a large area taken up by a football ground and by the self-esteem of the Marquesses of Bute (which required the 350 acres of Bute Park in which to stretch itself) there is nothing to be seen in the way of a city along this softly tree-lined riverbank. Such an extravagance of city-centre space deserves to have a better city spread around it.

By contrast, however, with the place as a whole, the Civic
Centre itself has an almost Parisian grandeur. It occupies
sixty acres of what was previously another park, and is spread
in this area with a fine balance between the white Portland-
stone buildings and the wide spaces in which they are set.
Now that the elms are reaching maturity and the buildings
have been cleaned we can, perhaps, see it at its best. It is so
much better than one could have hoped that it is tempting to
suppose that its success is accidental. But in fact it was a
product of its time (just as Swansea's Guildhall, which aims
for the same effect and fails, was of its). 1904 was the year of
its main construction.

The Civic Centre consists of a hierarchy of buildings,
administrative, legal, and educational. In the front row, and
presenting the facade for the whole complex, are three major,
separate but consistent items: the Law Courts, the City Hall,
and the National Museum. They each have, within an identity
of style, their own character and design.

The City Hall, in spite of its formal outward appearance, is
a busy, functioning building. Corridors and office doorways
abound, as in every council headquarters. The first floor of
the main hallway, however, is purely decorative. It contains
smooth, posed, marble statues of Welsh (or, since they
include Boudicca, British) worthies. It is rather an odd
collection, and, like so many things in Wales, weathered some
criticism when it came into being. The selection gives the
impression of a certain amount of barrel-scraping, and the
lifeless, ornamental poses preclude any great feeling of
national pride.

The next most notable building, alongside, and nearly as
prominent as the City Hall, is the Museum. As a building it
has a certain character and a good deal of splendour. As a
museum it largely sets out to instruct rather than to delight,
and consequently gets from bored school-children the noisy
disrespect which such an attitude deserves. The art section
contains a respectable, if modest, group of impressionists,
and acres of the usual landscapes and pastoral scenes by the
heavy traditionalists. Among the modern artists of Wales,
really only Augustus John (though by most standards hardly
modern) stands out at first sight as an authentic talent.

Outside the Museum, on a pedestal, stands David Lloyd George, furious as ever. Perhaps he is annoyed at not being put among the Ten Great Welshmen in the City Hall.

Apart from the several buildings of the University, the other major item of the Civic Centre is the building which has, since its creation in 1964, been the headquarters of the Welsh Office. The government department which has administered Wales during recent years operates from here and from offices in Whitehall, and has had control over almost every aspect of central government in Wales. Roads, housing, local government, everything significant except the Exchequer.

Though financial independence of England is probably technically possible, in that Wales could just about pay its way, it would be necessary for the whole country to accept, as a condition, a lower standard of living. This is to some a price worth paying for full freedom from English policies; the price, one might say, of the right to make one's own mistakes. To others the necessity is not so apparent, and many are satisfied with the degree of autonomy already obtained.

The question of Welsh independence has been discussed for many years. Lloyd George entered Parliament in 1890 with the firm intention of achieving not only Welsh disestablishment (which Gladstone's Liberal Party favoured) but complete Home Rule for Wales. A minor climax in the continuing campaign towards this ideal was reached in the autumn of 1973, with the publication of the report of the Royal Commission on the Constitution. The Kilbrandon commission recommended a directly-elected assembly for Wales:

Through such an assembly the aspirations and needs of the Welsh people would be fully discussed and formulated and made known to the United Kingdom Parliament and Government. Wales would be given the assurance it needs that its problems were being examined in sufficient depth and with adequate understanding.

They felt, however, that the idea of dividing Great Britain into three sovereign states seemed, to most people, quite absurd. What they recommended, in fact, was devolution of legislation and of executive powers in all regional matters. The suggestion was that specific matters, for this purpose, such as planning, local government, transport and education, should be transferred to the new assembly. These provisions, which still leave Wales financially supported by the overall British exchequer, go a long way towards satisfying the deep need which the nation has so long had, to be taken seriously as a country.

Though the Welsh Office has recently been the focus of administration, the country is not in fact governed entirely, or even mainly, through politics. The lines dividing one branch of activity from another are less clear in Wales than elsewhere, and the cultural, social and organizational spheres of Welsh life tend to merge. There are perhaps slightly less than a thousand people active, in one way or another, in running Wales. These, that is, are characterized by being not only prominent in their own lines but by thinking and acting in a national context – which may indeed, but often accidentally, spill over into England. They are all known to each other personally, and to everyone else by name, and there is no distinction among them of occupational hierarchy, as again there might well be elsewhere. Artists and politicians, educationists, journalists, architects, scientists, elder statesmen, all meet on an equal footing. They enjoy a sort of familiar fame, since though their status is national it is not a very large nation. Wales is, in fact, about the right-sized pond in which to be a fish of respectable dimensions.

The question in general of what defines the nation (a style of life, an attitude of mind?) never really arises, since the identity of the population pre-existed ideas of nationalism. The population of Cardiff, by contrast, has traditionally been largely immigrant. Butetown as it was (the Tiger bay of legend) was a crowded, busy slum-town full of Chinese eating-houses, gambling shops, doss-houses and brothels. A cataclysmic change overcame it during the 1960s and '70s. Now it has all come down, and Bute Street today presents a vast area of new housing very foreign, in its appearance, to the old image. Visibly it is a desert with houses in it. The old names, such as Loudon Square, look ridiculous on the walls of these trivial, anonymous buildings.

Behind this, however, something of the old spirit still survives. The communities deprived of their socially well-adapted terraced houses have stayed on in the tower blocks, and spread out again into these streets and streets of modern soullessness. And out at the back the children have taken over the planners' open spaces, devastating them with refuse and broken timber, painting their names heroicly on the walling, and building out of rubbish an elaborate play-world of climable, king-of-the-castle frameworks. In the distance the white pinnacle of the City Hall shines as a far-off irrelevant peak of another country, beyond their frontier. They have humanized the desert — and in so doing provided, unexpectedly, an argument in favour of dropping litter. Without the spread of debris which covers its ground like the foam of a sea Butetown today would be as utterly sterile as it was designed and built to be. By scattering the human, social element of rubbish over it the kids have relieved it of its facelessness.

It is, of course, unfair to wonder, as one unavoidably does, how it could have been done with so little spirit, so little feeling for the needs of a multi-racial, slum-based population. But how else could it have been done? One cannot build with anything other than a desire to provide better conditions, to raise the level of life towards respectability, with all the inevitable pressure towards embourgeoisement which this implies. Many of these third or fourth generation coloured Welshmen have received our standard education, and it must be assumed, in theory, that they are poised to become like the rest of us. One could not decently build-in the elements of degeneracy which once made Butetown what it was.

As it happens things do not work in this neat progressive way. The community has retained much of its independence and its traditions in the new surroundings. Prostitution flourishes still in the new suburban blocks, and no doubt if there were anywhere to put them the Chinese cafés and the doss-houses would creep back in. They carry on as before, but amid a different sort of squalor.

Particularly in the fringes of the area where some old back streets have not yet been pulled down, the essence of the spirit of Butetown as it was just survives, though with the last-stand aspect of something forced into a corner. Symptoms of it are the dirty-faced children in the pubs, the decrepits, the people with faces anciently or recently scarred by fights. And music. In times of canned and piped sensations it is something of a relief to know that, south of St John's Church and The Hayes, there are still people who know what music is for. They are, on the one hand, old ladies with even older pianos perpetuating a natural human tendency towards honky-tonk, delivering to a bar-room of down-at-heel drunks a stirring atmosphere of other times. And, on the other hand, increasingly exceptional cases of negro or multi-caste Cardiffians pounding out what would otherwise be schmaltz in a way that makes it an immediate part of anyone's existence.

Down beyond Butetown the Docks themselves retain, though probably for not much longer, some fragments of crumbling magnificence. Here and there amid the redevelopment one comes on vestiges of past splendour, indications of the wealth and exuberance of a place fully conscious of its greatness. A care about the architectural details combined with a sense of style made, once, places such as Mountstuart Square something a city could be proud of. The West Dock building outlived its contemporaries, elaborate and grandiose in red brick, but all the time with a forlorn expectation that it would eventually go the way of its counterpart across the road, demolished to make way for the Maritime Museum. The Docks in the meantime function as ever, but now no longer as an export base for coal. The bulk of the cargo now is coming in, rather than going out.

The Butes were largely personally responsible for the development of Cardiff as a port. The docks were, in fact, called Bute Docks, 165 acres developed from a starting date in 1839. The Butes came originally, of course, from Scotland, where their seat was (and still is) Mount Stuart Castle. One of them (the third Earl) rose to prominence in politics in the reign of George III, when, for a brief period in 1762, he replaced Pitt as prime minister. The ownership of Cardiff and of 25,000 acres of Glamorganshire was acquired by marriage to the heiress of the Earl of Pembroke. From then on, now elevated to the rank of Marquess, the Lords Bute lived in Cardiff Castle. They rebuilt it during the nineteenth and early twentieth centuries, and only finally left, to return to the Isle of Bute, in 1948, having given the castle to the Corporation.

The great expansion in the Bute fortune which Cardiff's success represented was due to the foresight of the second Marquess, who hazarded £350,000 of his personal fortune in building East Bute Dock in 1839. It was the almost instant success of this that enabled the third Marquess to undertake such a lavish restoration of the Castle (and indeed of several others in his possession) between 1865 and the mid 1870s.

The castle was of thoroughly respectable antiquity. It owes its origin to the Roman fort, the foundations of which can clearly be seen at the base of the great outer wall. The Marquess, in rebuilding, was careful to preserve the original, and since the Romans worked with lighter-coloured stone it is still quite easy to identify. Between it and the later work is a dividing line of darker stonework.

When the Normans entered Wales during the eleventh century to establish the Marcher Lordships, chief among them was Robert Fitzhamon, and his castle at Cardiff was the chief of the Norman castles which then sprang up. The keep which resulted from Fitzhamon's original motte and stockade still stands, as an effective centre-piece, in the north-west corner of the present rectangle of castle buildings. During the fourteenth and fifteenth centuries the castle expanded. Glendower's rebels took it in the early fifteenth, and Cromwell again overcame it in 1648. Some of the buildings of these periods are incorporated into the Butes' present reconstruction; other parts of the castle have been rebuilt completely.

The third Marquess's extravagant use of his wealth expresses itself in an equivalent extravagance of taste. The decorated rooms of the interior, now on view to the public, are preserved in the state which he created. They reveal an obsession with exotica and a lavishness of detail comparable to that which, fifty or sixty years later, found expression in Swansea's Brangwyn panels. To Bute, evidently, profusion was everything. No inch of the walls or ceilings, and in some cases the floors as well, was left undecorated. The result of so

much competition between ornamentations is that the only
general effect which comes over is one of claustrophobia. The
rooms, which are not very large, are made tiny and crowded
by the quantity of decorated detail which is crammed into
them. No doubt the Marquess was immensely proud of his
unstinting use of gold leaf and his importation of Arab
craftsmen to effect the rich Moorish designs. He would have
been very puzzled to hear us laughing.

We do not laugh, however, at his other, equally ridiculous,
product of whimsy, Castell Coch. Appearing in the distance
above the Pontypridd road out of Cardiff, it is inevitably a
surprise. It sits on its wooded hill so exactly as if perched
over the Rhine that one cannot but be impressed by the spirit
of impudence behind it, the imaginative extremism which
achieved not something fake or imitative, not a reference or
the adoption of a style, but a real complete romantic
medieval castle. It comes, like the German examples, not so
much from an age of military architecture, nor from a
particular part of the world, but straight out of the realm of
the imagination, which in its turn no doubt draws its source
material from the illustrations of children's book. Walt
Disney surely did not invent the fairytale castle, and one can
only suppose that John Patrick Crichton-Stuart, third
Marquess of Bute, and his architect William Burges, had, in
the middle of the last century, been brought up with notions
similar to our own.

Castell Coch was built in the 1870s. It occupied the site,
certainly, of an early castle, overlooking the lower Taff
valley. The siting of the castle there, at least, was not the
Marquess's idea; but there was very little left of the original
when Bute decided to rebuild, and what succeeded was, in its
entirety, the imaginative reconstruction of the earlier castle.
Although Burges made some efforts to justify his guesses
historically, it should not be thought that Castell Coch tells
us much, or is supposed to, about what a Welsh medieval
castle was actually like. It is a thing in its own right, and must
be appreciated as such.

In this light it is more successful than the equivalent
patron-and-architect collaboration at Cardiff. Castell Coch's

Tintern Abbey

interior decorations, in particular, are a great deal pleasanter to look at, because more sensitive and less extreme, and altogether in better taste in the sense that prettiness here predominates over showiness.

The castle is hard to reach, now that a major high-speed road tends to sweep one past it towards Pontypridd. It is perhaps best to take a road off to Tongwynlais, and search for it from there. On leaving its gates one may take a left-turn up an unmarked lane to pass by a back road through attractive woodland to Caerphilly.

If the qualification for being called a city is the possession of a cathedral, then Llandaff's claim to city status is greater than that of Cardiff. Fortunately the dilemma was avoided by the amalgamation, in 1922, of the two places. In spite of this, and of Llandaff's claims to cityship, the suburb of Cardiff which has the cathedral retains both its independence and its village character.

Llandaff's origins are very distant. It is mentioned as if well-known and well-established by both Giraldus and Geoffrey of Monmouth, in the mid-twelfth century. Although not much is known for certain, it is probable that St Teilo, during the middle of the sixth century, founded the first monastic settlement there. A twelfth-century Norman church, replacing a smaller and older one, forms the basis of the present building. Well-preserved and very splendid Norman arches still survive behind the altar and in the doorways. By about 1220 the building was substantially completed.

With the additon of the chapter-house the church was then considered finished, and was dedicated in 1266, about a hundred and forty years after it was started. The Lady Chapel, behind the altar, was added during the later part of the century, and, with its vaulting and its elegant Decorated window, is a fine example of that period's style.

Five hundred years later, however, it all seems to have been in a poor state of repair, since a storm brought down the south tower which, falling, crushed the medieval cleres-tory of the nave. For a time then (not for the last time) the great cathedral was a ruin. A rebuilding was started during

Llanthony Priory

the mid-eighteenth century under the hand of John Wood, whose obsession with the classical gave us the harmony and dignity of Bath, but threatened, at Llandaff, to destroy for ever the Gothic masterpieces which Wood ironically failed to appreciate. The work was never completed, and the classical temple which he had imposed on the eastern end of the cathedral was removed during the middle of the nineteenth century.

It was during that period, under a local architect, that the greatest restoration of the cathedral took place. A new tower and spire were built, and a new roof added to the old chapter-house. Much of this work, however, was undone, and had to be done all over again; on 2nd January 1941, a bomb fell close to the cathedral and completely shattered it.

Restoration was once again undertaken during the 1950s, and one significant addition made to the nave. Now this innovation, startling and impressive, dominates the view of the inside as one comes down into it. It is not so much the double arches of reinforced concrete, forming a symbolic rood screen across the church; it is the tall and thin hanging figure of Christ on the organ case above the arches which monopolizes one's first impression. By its great size and striking proportions Epstein's 'Christ in Majesty' quite overwhelms the interior of the church. Its cast aluminium surface is well set-off by the simple concrete structure which supports it.

The whole effect created by this sound use of materials is unfortunately slightly spoilt by the intrusion of a different scale, material, and colour, in the form of 64 gold figures (saints and angels) which are attached to the organ case. They were the figures placed in the niches of the choir stalls by the nineteenth-century restorers. In themselves they are, (like the creation panels in one of the chapels and the Triptych by Rossetti in another, which were additions of the same period), fine and artistic works. It is a pity they should have been so inappropriately placed on this huge, soaring, modern structure.

The rural setting of Llandaff gives to the small cathedral a feeling of peace and ease. The atmosphere spreads around it, the village fortunately remaining a backwater secluded from that hubbub of roads which makes the outskirts of Cardiff so tense an experience. Llandaff miraculously retains its village character. It has kept its scale and its sense of values.

These two factors, scale and values, are predominant features of the other notable attraction of this area, St Fagan's Folk Museum. The idea of a national Folk Museum – displaying the rural physical culture characteristic of the traditional community – is by no means new. A successful one has been in operation outside Oslo for some decades. St Fagan's itself came into existence in the 1940s, grew during the 1950s, and recently, in the '70s, has undergone a major expansion of facilities, involving the construction of several new buildings. These new constructions provide exhibition space which is more of the nature of a regular museum. What is much more fascinating about St Fagan's, of course, is the old buildings and their impedimenta.

The re-erected buildings have been brought from all parts of Wales, and cover both a range of styles and a stretch of centuries which present a representative view of old things and old modes of life in Wales. The total selectiveness of the scene (in which everything is old and small) gives at first a rather eerie feeling – that of being in a real world which is somehow not real, as if in a dream or under a spell.

The buidings sit as though naturally in hollows and glades. There are flowers and beans in the gardens, and sheep graze in the fields. What is absent is the activity; and the lack of clanking and shouting, of the streak of sheep-dogs and the rising of smoke from the chimneys, throws over the whole thing a middle-of-the-night strangeness. Moreover it is all too neat and clean to be quite real. What one gets is an objective, external, God's-eye-view of these human contexts: the physical surroundings without the involvement of human presences. Everything is there except the subjective meaning, the filter of real-life which would make it all look different. Though we can note (which they would not have done) the cruck trusses and wattle walls, we are not entirely able to feel what it would all have been like.

Clearly life would not have been so lovely, bright and clean and smelling of furniture polish. One misses the hovel-

dweller's tang of squalor; the cats and the smell of dung from
the yard, the fluster of poultry. Real farm-houses in Wales
have in their back-rooms the enclosing smell of clothes and
cooking, and a chaos of grime-faced children. And in the
parlour the stale air of a closed and seldom-used room, the
deadened willow-pattern world of spotless formality.

St Fagan's was once a medieval castle, but it fell into
disrepair at an early date, and a fine Elizabethan house was
built on its site. This now stands, as part of the museum, in
its formal gardens falling in terraces to a series of ponds. The
new buildings, near the car-park, include the intimidatingly-
tilted Gallery of Material Culture, where an awesome
dissection of the physical daily lives of the nation, as a
nation, is set out. It views the people not as people but as
representatives of Welsh-ness, and so has a slightly inhuman
atmosphere. All the bits and pieces associated with the
activities of the Welsh are laid out in evidence.

In this north and north-western direction Cardiff quickly
opens out into pleasant countryside. Not so to the east,
where it practically merges with Newport. Much new housing
fills the hinterland between them. Newport, however, remains a town in its own right, a commercial and industrial
centre of more than 100,000 people. It is on the Usk, at the
terminus of the Monmouthshire canal, and owes its rise and
subsequent importance largely to its docks. As a port, there is
nothing really new about it; Giraldus mentions it by name,
and up to his time it was known as Novus Burgus, being an
offshoot, down river, of Caerleon.

Here, as everywhere, there is a Norman castle; but the
remnants of it here are overwhelmed by the larger scale of
urbanization. Newport roars and streams around it, a noisy
and congested place the normal mode of which is expressed
by the rattle of pneumatic drills and the gurgle of the engines
of buses. One old sixteenth-century house in the High Street
sits incongruously among the twentieth-century commercial
architecture and the traffic fumes. Its quiet and plaintive
message, quite failing to compete with the uproar, is:
Newport was not always like this.

It rose to prominence only after the construction of the

Docks, in 1842. Though it had been a borough since 1624, its
population at the start of the nineteenth century was only
just over a thousand. Now, however, it is hard to separate it
in imagination from the world of bingo and motorbikes,
road-repairs, and multi-storey carparks.

There is, however, the haven of the Kingsway Centre, a
very large covered shopping complex which includes, among
its many pleasant features, a museum, library, and art gallery.
The tensive effects of the presence of cars removed, the
walkways among the shops recreate a human atmosphere,
where people become one again of significance. Outside, they
are hinderances to the traffic. Through the galleries of the
two-level shopping precinct music replaces the nervous noise,
a fact which perhaps adds to this sudden sense of easing.
Elsewhere in Newport life is anything but beautiful, and in
many ways it is perhaps as well that few, if any, of the
scurrying people in the streets have time to stand and stare.

W. H. Davies's poem "Leisure" – "What is this life if, full
of care . . ." – is perhaps the thing for which he is most
famous, but is in fact only one of his many pleasant and
unpretentious verses. William Henry Davies is probably
Newport's only famous son, born in a pub there in the year
1871. When he was 22 he emigrated to America, and
travelled as a tramp in that then emergent country for some
years. He lost a leg while trying to jump a train, and the
equanimity with which he accepted this incident, and
recounted it in his *Autobiography*, is characteristic of his
straightforward attitude to everything:

Even then I did not know what had happened, for I attempted to
stand, but found that something had happened to prevent me from
doing this. Sitting down in an upright position, I then began to
examine myself, and now found that the right foot was severed from
the ankle.

Davies was, and considered himself, a poet. His poems are
largely observations of nature, quiet in tone and with a
timeless directness. He was given much encouragement by the
poet Edward Thomas, and a volume of his poetry impressed
George Bernard Shaw. The result was that when Thomas

persuaded him to write his autobiography Shaw was willing
to add a Preface. Such was Shaw's status at the time that *The
Autobiography of a Super-Tramp* was assured success, but
even so one is tempted to think that its quality would in any
case have been recognized. The clarity of mind and honesty
of the work mark it as an exceptional record. The prose too
is as quite uncluttered with pretention as is the attitude.
There is nothing second-hand about it, no romantic posing
for the benefit of public expectations. As Shaw says
succinctly, you never suspect him of having read *Lavengro*.

Davies returned once or twice between journeys to his
native town; he gave up tramping eventually to spend all his
time on poetry, lived a settled life in Gloucestershire, and
died in 1940.

Newport has one remarkable object of interest, besides the
forlorn castle and the enterprising Kingsway Centre. The Usk
below the town is bridged by a huge and elaborate
concoction known as the Transporter Bridge. It is an aerial
ferry, a positively draconian way of attacking the obstacle of
the mild muddy river. A huge construction suspends, by a
cat's-cradle of cables, a hanging platform which slowly,
purposefully, transports a few cars over the water. The
justification for this elaborate procedure, presumably, is that
it avoids interference with shipping, while not requiring the
road to rise higher than its normal level. The bridge, which
has a span of 645 feet, was opened in 1906, and has much of
the fine character, architecturally, of the period of seaside
piers and railway stations. The element of absurdity (the
largeness of the undertaking and the smallness of the task)
contributes to this character.

Newport has, below the Transporter Bridge, a very
extensive area of docks. Flat and exposed, beside the tidal
Usk, the place is bleak, like all such uninhabited terrains: a
plain of railway lines and a forest of cranes.

PART SIX

GWENT

XIV   THE USK

It would be wrong to assume that the flow of water between
England and Wales (that controversial export) goes all one
way. Much of Wales's water in fact comes out of England,
in the form of streams and tributaries which eventually
make up the rivers Wye and Monnow. The Monnow rises on
the hills which face the Black Mountains across the Honddu
valley, those furrowed slopes which form the wide block of
beautiful country to the west of Hereford. The Usk is
actually respectably Welsh in its source, coming as it does out
of the heart of the Brecon Beacons. The Wye originates north
of Builth Wells, but emigrates at Hay to wander in a long,
relaxed loop through the Herefordshire fields, where, under
those wild oaks and hedgerow trees, it gathers much of its
strength.

What a magnificent country Britain is, having on the banks
of one of its rivers alone the fine cattle-lands of Herefordshire
and the good Radnorshire sheep pastures. The town of
Hay-on-Wye reflects this sound quality, being a solidly-
established town the chief focus of which is its agricultural
market. One could hardly fail to feel the mood of farming
which pervades the place, with its warehouses and cattle-
trucks and the gum-booted tread of its people.

Like so many towns in this corner of Wales, Hay has its
crumbling ruin, the fat-walled Norman castle which overlooks
it. One would, in fact, by now feel that something was
missing from any reasonably substantial South Wales town
which had not got this piece of scenery, a civic amenity
which forms an unnoticed background to the busy streets. In
the case of Hay, the castle is perhaps more ruined than most,
and of rather less historical interest. It was converted to a

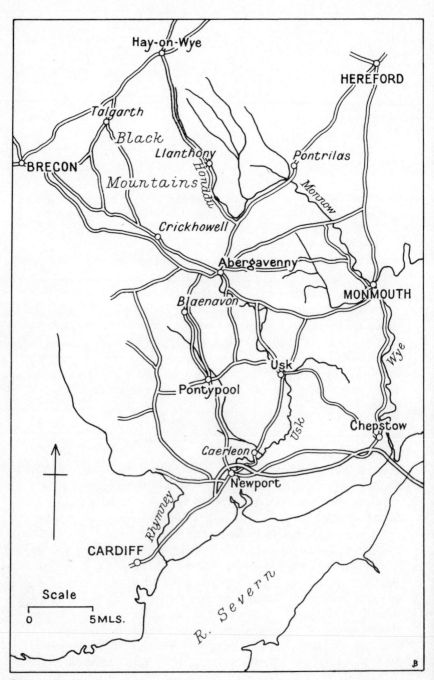

Gwent

fortified manor during Tudor times and the hybrid building was later gutted by fire.

Hay-on-Wye is only just in Wales. The border, in the form of the Dulas brook, wanders round the edge of the town. But, hard as it would be to analyse, the character of the place is clearly Welsh. It is, perhaps, something about its complexity, its many-faceted appearance. And from here there is not much doubt about the rising, tumbling countryside, where the road (with, in this direction, no choice) runs south, rising first out of the river valley and onto open hillsides.

The lane – it can hardly be called a road – flows down from this watershed among the wrinkled hills and over open moorland. But the Ewyas valley, into which it falls, is not for lovers of deserts. This is now no wilderness, but a thickly vegetated country. Dense scrub of oak and hazel crowds the roads, and the outlook onto the narrow river valley is all green with small fields and their thick hedges. There never was so bosky a valley as the Ewyas, in the depths of which the Honddu stream and the only road of the eastern flanks of the Black Mountains run together towards Llanthony.

Llanthony lies in the fields, at a point at which the valley has, unobtrusively, slightly widened and opened the views of its slopes. The ruins of the Priory standing in this overwhelmingly rural setting exert a considerable evocation of peace, of peacefulness and the sort of attitude that goes with it.

The name – which is pronounced Llan Tony – is a corruption (current by the end of the twelfth century) of the original form Llan Nant Hodeni, after the river (now called Honddu) which runs past it.

The Priory was first built in 1107, and what stands today dates largely from that century. A part of it was converted at an early date to become a hotel, which it still is: the southern tower and the buildings around it. During its prime the abbey served as a retreat for many prominent people of that medieval period. The Augustinian monks actually departed, presumably because of border warfare in the unsettled times of King Stephen, to another Llanthony outside Gloucester. Giraldus regretted the extent to which, even by his time, "the step-daughter had supplanted her mother". He drew some comfort from the thought that Llanthony might, by the withdrawal, be relieved of worldly affairs and return to the contemplation for which it was so fitted.

Let the active reside there, the contemplative here; there the pursuit of terrestrial riches, here the love of celestial delights; there let them enjoy the concourse of men, here the presence of angels.

And although the Augustinians had not abandoned the Priory entirely, keeping a small community of monks there, (gradually dwindling until only five were left), the place was in a run-down state, and probably growing beyond repair, by the time of the Dissolution of the Monasteries.

Since then Llanthony has always been in private hands. It is in private ownership now, and the hotel which has provided hospitality through the centuries is still inhabited. For a time after the Dissolution of the Monasteries it was used as a hunting lodge. In 1802 it was acquired, along with the whole valley, by Walter Savage Landor, who spent much wealth and wasted much effort on an experiment in social and agricultural improvements there, which he abandoned after only six years, when the difficulties which he had by then got himself into forced him to live abroad. The family at present in occupation of the Priory and hotel bought it from the Landor estate, of whom they were the tenants, and have been in residence more than a hundred years.

In so far as he is known now at all, Landor is perhaps best known for the short poem he wrote very late in his long life.

I strove with none, for none was worth my strife;
Nature I loved and, next to Nature, Art:
I warmed both hands before the fire of life,
It sinks, and I am ready to depart.

The first line is simply quite untrue. Landor was noted for his violent temper and hot-headed ways.

Perhaps it is these personal connections which make Llanthony so sympathetic. It is, as ruins unfortunately must be, cared for by the Ministry of Works (now a branch of the Department of the Environment), and they have applied to it, in places, that standardization process with which they so frequently assassinate our ancient buildings. But the lawns and peacocks still convey an intimate and human feeling, in keeping with the neat and unpretentious proportions of the ruins themselves. Llanthony is not small; one only has to stand at one end of the nave and look down its full extent to realize that it was a very sizeable church. But compared to the over-bearing magnificence of Tintern, for instance, it is of comprehensible dimensions, and something of this unaggressive harmony, perhaps, goes towards making it the instrument of tranquility which it is.

This amazing peace which floods the Ewyas valley is at its strongest at Cwmyoy, a tiny dozing village on the valley slope. The fairy-story unreality of it is heightened by the absurd crookedness of its small church, which juts at every angle except the vertical and horizontal. It was the bad luck of the church of St Martin at Cwmyoy to be built on a rock-fault, which, by landslips and subsidence over the centuries since it was built, has tilted and twisted it into its present crazy shape.

The Honddu out of the Vale of Ewyas joins the Monnow and its tributaries, which all turn north together to loop around the top of this chapter and flow down into the next one. One suspects them of having, at some time, changed their course; in the valley which opens at Llanfihangel Crucorney as if to receive them, only the insignificant Gavenny stream appears.

The Gavenny would, that is, be of no significance, if it were not the origin of that well-known place name. The use of 'Aber' here, in the name Abergavenny, in its meaning of 'confluence', is unusual in Wales as a whole, although there are several examples of it in the river valleys of the south. Normally it refers to the confluence of a river with the sea, and almost every Aber in mid and north Wales is on an estuary. Here Abergavenny marks the spot at which the Gavenny runs into the Usk.

From the Usk valley there is an appearance of background hills, giving no clue that Abergavenny sits at their feet, under, on the one hand, the clear symmetrical outline of the Sugar Loaf, and, on the other, the hump of Skirrid Fawr.

Abergavenny is of remarkably solid antiquity. The site of, originally, the castle of the giant Agros, it later formed one of the Romans' inroads into the tribal hill-country of Gwent, at which point of history it was called Gobannium. A Norman castle inevitably followed. "The castle of Abergevenni," Giraldus mentions, "is so called from its situation at the confluence of the river Gevenni with the Usk." It was apparently in the decade before Giraldus's visit that a famous act of treachery (or, according to one's viewpoint, revenge) took place in the early Norman motte-and-bailey castle which formerly occupied the site of the present ruins. Hollinshed describes the event:

> A.D.1176, The same yeare, William de Breause having got a great number of Welshmen into the castle of Abergavennie, under a colourable pretext of communication, proposed this ordinance to be received of them with a corporall oth, "that no traveller by the waie amongst them should beare any bow, or other unlawful weapon," which oth, when they refused to take, because they would not stand to that ordinance, he condemned them all to death. This deceit he used towards them, in revenge of the death of his uncle Henrie of Hereford, whom upon Easter-even before they had through treason murthered, and were now acquited was the like againe.

Giraldus diplomatically tries to skirt this issue, saying "We leave to others the relation of those frequent and cruel excesses which in our times have arisen among the inhabitants of these parts, against the governors or castles, and the indictive retaliations of the governors against the natives." With his tendency to scandal-mongering he is obviously very tempted to be more specific about what it is he is not going to tell us, but repeats that he thinks it better to omit "the enormous cruelties and slaughter perpetrated here in our days . . . lest bad men should be induced to follow the example."

Abergavenny next appears in Churchyard's rhyming gazetteer, *The Worthiness of Wales*, where a catalogue of the people buried at the church is given in considerable jingling detail. The church, originally a Benedictine priory founded by the Norman lord Hamelin de Baladun, who built the castle, contains some fine effigies, brasses, and decorated choir stalls.

Much of what remains of the castle (chiefly, that is, the gatehouse) is of the fourteenth century. Its ruins now form the framework for a pleasant public garden, and one extreme of this looks down over the wide Usk valley.

What is perhaps more remarkable about Abergavenny is that all this history is quite unobservable in the apparent fact, which by contrast is simply that of a solid and unpretentious town of some 10,000 people, minding its own business in a corner of the valley under the mild hills. It looks, and is, a standard, not specially beautiful, Welsh town, with one main street, occasional Georgian and Victorian house-fronts, surrounded by sedate residential suburbs from the earlier decades of this century. It is Welsh by character, but, like all the border country, utterly English by language — the thick, soft accent is not even definitely a Welsh one, but a blend of Hereford and Gloucester, with an occasional South-Wales lift. The most notable feature of the town, and perhaps the one thing which makes it at all remarkable, is the huge covered market with its conspicuous tower.

The countryside around Abergavenny is perhaps best characterized by the pretty villages of Rockfield and Llantilio Crossenny, which are tiny and very rural places, set in a complicated landscape of streams and winding lanes. Southward the Usk and the A40 flow, dividing at Llanfihangel Gobion, the one to go to Usk and Caerleon, the other to Raglan. A considerable network of roads now sweeps around the Raglan area, hurrying people from one motorway to another. Raglan village is consequently left lying on its own, like an ox-bow lake, looking a little purposeless. It is divided from its castle by a furious river of traffic, which impatiently ignores them both.

The Normans moved very swiftly into South Wales, and this ring of castles — Abergavenny, Monmouth, Chepstow, Caerleon, and Usk — came into being during the late 1060s and early 1070s, to be substantially completed, in their early form, within ten years of the Norman Conquest's famous date. Raglan forms a junction of ways between the points of the ring, and it is highly likely that a fortress there arose at the same time. What we see there now, however, is all of later date, none of it being earlier than the fifteenth century. Its shape and layout, together with the importance of its site, make it seem almost certain that the present buildings occupy the same position as an earlier Norman fortress, which would perhaps have been made of wood.

Raglan today exudes an atmosphere of great power and wealth, an impression which is not at all misleading, since it was, in its present form, the family seat of the Herbert family (the Earls of Pembroke and later of Huntingdon and Worcester) from the middle of the fifteenth century onwards. Its comparatively late date of building has given it sophistications which the cruder medieval castles (which, in Wales, are so familiar) lack. Built in a time of innovation, after the widespread use of gunpowder and hence of cannons in the sieging and defence of castles, it incorporates in its design both the old and the new. Gun-ports, for instance, supplement the traditional arrow-slits.

Perhaps the most striking physical feature of the castle is the Great Tower, traditionally called the Yellow Tower of Gwent, which stands in the midst of the defensive system, and yet somehow apart, a unit within a unit, both part of the castle and a castle on its own. Designed as self-contained – it had, it seems, provision for a kitchen in the basement – it was clearly intended, in the manner of a keep, as a last defence, a stronghold to which the family could retreat when the rest of the castle had fallen and still be safe.

Much of the rest of the castle appears now, with its fine high mullioned windows and its plentiful provision of living rooms – gallery, hall, dining-room and parlour – to be exactly what it was: an Elizabethan family house, built on a very grand scale indeed. Its glory survived into Stuart times, when Charles I, it is said, played bowls on the still immaculate green above the moat, in the climactic summer of 1645. And the splendour only came to an end, with so much else, when Charles's game of bowls was over and the world became a different place.

Throughout history there has never been a time when money and politics did not lie close together, and then, in the seventeenth century, as ever, great wealth and political power tended to reside in the same people. The enormous riches of the Herberts caused them to become, effectively, the

Royalists' bank. The Earl of Worcester, then the head of the house, garrisoned Raglan for the king at his own cost, amounting to some £40,000 in that day's currency. Charles was subsidized further by the Herberts to the amount, it was claimed, of about a million pounds, a fortune indeed for the mid-seventeenth century. Raglan consequently became a Royalist headquarters, and the house, which had by then become so much a dwelling-place, reverted to its natural status of castle.

Charles, who had played his bowls at Raglan in July, after the defeat at Naseby but before the beginning of complete despair, was there again in time to hear of the fall of Bristol in September, 1645. The siege of Raglan itself began the next summer, and it was battered by Colonel Morgan and some 5,000 men, together with the full force of Parliament's skill and equipment, for two and a half months. By the end of that time Fairfax himself, Cromwell's commander-in-chief, had joined the siege, a testimony to the importance attached to the taking of Raglan. When it fell, on 19th August, the Civil War was in effect over.

The immediate and most conspicuous result of this was that Raglan castle was then virtually demolished. That is, what was by then left of it, after its long and constant battering. We are lucky indeed to have as much of it left as we have, and only the strength with which it had been built up over so long a period prevented the Cromwellians destroying it entirely. Demolition continued throughout the next century, the family, by then restored to their owner-ship, using Raglan as a source of material for their other properties. In view of all this it is amazing that Raglan still contains so much of an air of its original grand state. Only one item, perhaps, remains of so striking a kind as to show just how grand this was. A fragment of a carved chimney-piece on the gallery wall. Looking up at it, among so much bare stone and gaunt outlines of walls, one catches the sudden and poignant whiff of the Renaissance.

And that is what it is, this aura around Raglan. That is what makes one feel that this is not, as so many of the great castles of Wales seem to be, a tribute to the austerity and stoicism of men who were harder and braver than we are, living in hard times and holding their lives cheaply. Raglan, uniquely, is a castle one could live in. It has about it, like some great country houses, an air of civilized pleasures. One feels it was inhabited by people who liked good things and probably completely lacked vulgarity. But the contrast is an even more embracing one; that step from Conway to Raglan, from the dogmatic Middle Ages to the subtlety of Renaissance times, is from the obscurity of things which are beyond our understanding and into the clarity of times which are the actual background to our own. Raglan is, in a way, part of our thinking.

Alternatively to this road past Raglan, a smaller road goes south, beside the river, to pass through the town of Usk itself, which is a small, pleasant and unremarkable place at the river crossing. The town is frequented by salmon fishers, an attribute which gives it better hotels than such a village would normally possess, and its streets tend to ring, at any rate in times of spate, with those tweed voices which so often go with fishing. It lies in the valley bottom, river-oriented, proud of its wide-spanning bridge and its pretty little square, overlooked by a crumbling castle in the trees. The wide brown river there runs shallowly over its stones.

The Usk valley, in contrast to the Wye, is wide and rather shapeless. It makes for good agriculture but only moderate scenery, and the level fields of its sandy soil stretch, with their grazing Herefords, all the way from Usk to Caerleon.

The same river flows through Caerleon. Caerleon: Castra Legionum. The name greatly pre-dates even those misty sources of British mythology thanks to which it is best known. It became famous in the Middle Ages because it was already famous, and by resorting to the literature, rather than by looking on the ground, one can even now see why.

The facts are these — and they underlie the fiction rather as an invisible groundwork of paint underlies an Old Master. Isca, a fort on a bend of the Usk, from which (in the manner of most Roman camps) it took its name, was first founded in around A.D. 75 as a base for the Second Augustan Legion. The massive attack on the Silures, a hill tribe with, very probably, winter pastures on the coastal plain, was thus given a centre. An iron-age hillfort a mile to the north-west shows the sort of thing the attack from Caerleon was concerned with. It formed a base from which the field-forts at Neath, Carmarthen and Brecon could be supported. It remained in use until the Second Legion became involved, in the late fourth century, with the Saxon invasions, (being removed, it is thought, to Richborough), and was evacuated in about the year 375. By this time one must assume that the Silures had been tamed, becoming fully-Romanized Britons, since a civil settlement then replaced the fort near the river.

At its prime the fort accommodated nearly 6,000 men, and occupied an area of fifty acres. The Amphitheatre, which is perhaps its most visible remaining feature, was erected around A.D. 80, and underwent repairs in the early third century. It fell into disuse from the fourth century on. A public display area such as this would be used not only for the sort of entertainment which one associates with the time of bread and circuses, but, very largely, for military demonstrations and drill.

It can be seen from these brief facts that Roman Caerleon constituted something very much more substantial than the few lines of masonry among the grass (which, by looking rather hard, one can still find today) would suggest. The Parish Church — a sixth-century foundation, dedicated to St Cadoc, which today contains, at the south-west end of the nave, a Norman arch, which is its oldest feature — stands at the geographical centre of the fort site, which therefore spread over much of what is now the town. A great deal of it was left, embellished either by the art of the early Middle Ages or by the imaginations of its recorders, when Geoffrey of Monmouth and Giraldus wrote about it in the twelfth century. Geoffrey, in fact, felt it to be so prominent among the sites of ancient Britain that he made it the chief seat of his hero, Arthur. He even gave it a respectable British, pre-Roman, history, attributing its foundation to the mythical god-king Belinus.

Among the others which he founded was a certain city on the bank of the River Usk, near to the Severn Sea: this was the capital of Demetia and for a long time it was called Kaerusc. When the Romans

came the earlier name was dropped and it was re-named the City of
the Legions ...

And so when Arthur held court and received the homage
of other kings, it was at Caerleon that he did it, which
Geoffrey then describes in some detail.

On the other sie, which was flanked by meadows and wooded
groves, they had adorned the city with royal palaces, and by the
gold-painted gables of its roofs it was a match for Rome.

If we are to believe Giraldus, these gold-painted roofs seem
actually to have existed, and the remains of them were
probably there, decorating the medieval town which had
grown out of the Roman civil settlement, for Geoffrey and, a
few decades later, for Giraldus to see for themselves. Gerald
says:

Many vestiges of its former splendour may yet be seen; immense
palaces, formerly ornamented with gilded roofs, in imitation of
Roman magnificence ...

And he goes on to describe the baths, aqueducts, and
heating systems, which, even more, seem likely to be
authentic relics of the Roman city.

There is evidence, of course, that, as we immediately
suspect, Giraldus had been reading Geoffrey; and also that
the compilers of the *Mabinogion* (that rather later work
which gathers up, and saves for us, most of what was left by
then of British myth), had been reading both. The association
of Arthur with important Roman sites is common enough,
and could be explained, even if Geoffrey's influence were not
sufficient explanation, by the nature of the places: ancient
stones, pre-existing even the long traditions of local memory,
about which the population must inevitably be entirely
ignorant. Arthur, by definition, belonged to a previous age,
and so did the Romans. Given the vague idea of chronology
which people other than historians have always had, it is
hardly surprising that they should find themselves together.

We read, for instance, in the tale of "Geraint son of
Erbin":

It was Arthur's custom to hold court at Caer Lion on Usk ... for
Caer Lion was the most accessible place in his dominions, by sea and
by land.

Whatever the former glory of the place may once have
been, there is remarkably little sign of it there today. A quiet
and respectable town lies beside the tidal river Usk. Traffic
churns around it. To one side, on an open and featureless
piece of level ground, the Roman ruins sit inconspicuously:
low, square walls of meaningless cubicles, and the grassy
banks of the sunken amphitheatre. Amazingly even the tingle
of mystery has completely gone from it all.

Much more evocative, and much less praised and described
by ancient writers, is the similarly vanished city of Venta
Silurum, the site of which, at Caerwent, allows one to
imagine a large and solid Roman town, on a slight rise of the
rolling land. The suburbs of Newport sprawl outwards
between the two places, with the ever-present threat of
further urban floods bursting over Monmouthshire; but
Caerwent and Caerleon, only a few miles apart, are closely
related.

Built at about the same time, A.D. 75, Caerwent is unusual
in being much more of a civil settlement than a fort. It
remained inhabited, though decreasingly, until the mid fifth
century. It was built, it seems likely, to rehouse the
population of the hill-fort which overlooks it from Llanmelin
woods, which, strengthened in the early period of the Roman
occupation, was defeated and abandoned – probably as a
consequence of the building, in such a key position, of
Caerleon. The tribe was removed from its hill-fort, but
allowed to retain its identity, and became, settled at
Caerwent, a Roman subject-nation. One wonders how the
Silures took to their new home on the plain, under the eye of
the Roman army.

Within the huge square of the Roman walls (amounting to
about 44 acres) most of the present town of Caerwent
sits – the pub, the church, the small brown cottages,
orchards and grazing cattle, and the small bustle of its one
short street. The well-preserved bases of the walls look out
over the fields. Life was probably quite good in Venta

Silurum, if the area was then anything like the mild country place which it is today.

XV   THE WYE

Out of the broad and generalized agricultural acres, and into a more intimate countryside, with wooded slopes and broken horizons, runs the Wye valley and the way to Monmouth. The great roads go sweeping on to more important places, and we are in country-lane land, pitching down into the villages of stream valleys, veering round the corners of people's houses, disturbing a dog or two, always subordinate to the nature-dominated surroundings. The outlook is cluttered and small-scale, bounded by copses and escarpments, and that, as much as anything else, is why it seems like Wales.

Monmouth and Monmouthshire are so obviously Welsh that it seems odd that there should ever have been any doubt about this point; and although the border runs very close around the town, and sweeps in its dogmatic way down that lovely valley, it is easy all the time to feel that one is deep in the country's distinctive heart.

Monmouth is a gracefully sprawling town in the arms of two rivers, the hurrying Monnow and the languid Wye. The town has several remarkable physical features, best of which, is of course, its very pretty bridge-gatehouse, a rare (and in Britain at least, unique) example of a fortified medieval bridge. It was erected in the mid-thirteenth century. A wide cattle market stretches nearby, beside the Monnow, providing a mark of the town's primary character.

The Shire Hall in the main square, with its fine civic frontage under which the market stalls carry on their busy mornings, an eighteenth-century building which possesses to the full the good manners and self-confidence of that century, perhaps gives Monmouth its main distinction. In front of it, one in a niche and the other on a pedestal, stand two figures, the one in armour and holding a sceptre, the other, with a cap on, holding an aeroplane. The latter is

Charles Stewart Rolls, and the former, impressive in his gold crown, is Henry V, who was born, in 1387, in Monmouth Castle. His father, Henry Bolingbroke, who was, by deposing Richard II, to become Henry IV, was not then king, and no one at that point would have been able to foresee the events which were largely consequences of his usurpation – Glendower's rebellion, Prince Henry's rise to prominence, and the great military career which ultimately led to the naming of this central square in Monmouth 'Agincourt Square'.

The other figure commemorated in the square was not actually born in Monmouth, but had family connections with the vicinity. He was the son of Lord Llangattock, and would perhaps not be quite so worthy of being on a plinth in Agincourt Square if he had not, in 1906, joined the firm of F.H. Royce & Co. at Manchester. Originally an electrical and engineering business, this firm was by then pioneering motor car construction. Together Rolls and Frederick Royce founded a firm called Rolls-Royce Ltd., in Derby, with Rolls (who had become a car enthusiast while still an undergraduate at Cambridge) as chief engineer. The firm prospered under Royce; but Rolls, who had turned his attention to aeroplanes, became the first Englishman to be killed in a flying accident, when, in Bournemouth in 1910, the tail of his machine went wrong while he was participating in a flying competition.

Monmouth's other striking building is the long, curved Market Hall, which now houses mainly the town's Post Office. It was originally built in 1837, but rebuilt, after being badly damaged by fire, in the early 1960s.

This one-armed man with the eyepatch is following us around. The Post Office building also houses a Nelson Museum, and, so far from the sea, one might well wonder why. Nelson did happen to visit the town in 1802, casting one approving eye over the preposterous 'Naval Temple' built (in 1800) on top of the Kymin, a fine outlook behind the town. But the relics in the Nelson Museum actually represent the hobby of a leading Nelson enthusiast, none other than Lady Llangattock, the mother of Charles Rolls.

Monmouth's other famous son (if one discounts Shakespeare's Fluellen, who makes such claims for Monmouth that one might suspect that he too was a native) is perhaps the one mainly responsible for the widespread familiarity of the town's name. Geoffrey Arthur, who wrote that rambling and often ridiculous work, *The History of the Kings of Britain*, called himself Gaufridus Monemutensis, that is, Geoffrey of Monmouth, and it seems quite certain that he was born in Monmouth about the turn of the eleventh to twelfth centuries. He has been known to us down the centuries as Geoffrey of Monmouth, and although there is no knowledge of any connection that he had with the town besides originating from it, the fact that he chose to call himself after it at least indicates that it was a well-known and respectable place even then.

Goeffrey Arthur (as his name in fact was) was an academic cleric probably based on Oxford. In 1151 he was made Bishop of St Asaph, in North Wales, but it is likely that he never actually visited his See. The *History* (published in 1136) is far from being historical, and although he claimed to be working from "a very ancient book", and although some of his material can be traced to such identifiable sources as Nennius's *Historia Brittonum*, a large part of what he wrote was in all probability his own invention. It would in fact not be too great an exaggeration to say that he thus invented, single-handed, the bulk of British mythology in its final form. Whatever the remoter origins of the stories and characters, they come down to us now as distorted by Geoffrey's imagination.

The work sets out to trace the history of the people of Britain. Of where?

Britain, the best of islands, is situated in the Western Ocean, between France and Ireland. It stretches for eight hundred miles in length and for two hundred in breadth. It provides in unfailing plenty everything that is suited to the use of human beings. It abounds in every kind of mineral. It has broad fields and hillsides which are suitable for the most intensive farming and in which, because of the richness of the soil, all kinds of crops are grown in their season. It also has open woodlands which are filled with every kind of game.

The ancestry of the kings of Britain is traced back to a

certain Brutus, great-grandson of Aeneas the Trojan. Mythical figures of the native tradition, probably originally pre-Roman British gods, such as Bladud and Leir, Belinus, Brennius and Lud, feature in the succession up to the Roman invasion. Not all of this either came out of nowhere or disappeared back into obscurity, since fragments of continuing tradition echo Geoffrey's tales. He tells us the story of King Lear, or Leir, and his three daughters; and mentions that a gate of the city of London is called after the city's founder, King Lud. as indeed it still is. The Roman occupation and eventual withdrawal occupy the next long central section.

The book then really comes into its own with the arrival on the national scene of his two main heroes, Merlin and Arthur. While the former was almost entirely Geoffrey's own creation, Arthur too would probably have remained an obscure and minor leader of the troubled times of invasion and resistance, if this work had not built him up into something very much more: a king, an Emperor, a focus for nationalistic pride and a peg for romantic and heroic stories.

The effort was not wasted, and the *History* quickly became a major influence in European literature. There can be little doubt that it is largely responsible for the sudden blossoming of interest in Arthurian romance during the twelfth century, providing a climate of taste which facilitated the popularity of, among other great works, the poems of Chrétien de Troyes. The "Matter of Britain" has flowed on ever since, its continental ramifications being gathered up again three centuries later in Malory's magnificent *Morte d'Arthur*, but it was Geoffrey of Monmouth's long *History*, crude and rambling as it is, which first set the snowball rolling.

Monmouth Castle, where Henry V was born, is now a hardly visible fragment, of which it is difficult to find even a view. It was first built in 1071, as part of that rapid and conclusive invasion of this side of South Wales by the Norman Lords. In a sort of inversion of what one would expect to be the normal course of events, it fell out of private hands and into the ownership of the Crown during the thirteenth century. In the time of Henry III it then became a property of the Earl of Lancaster, which would explain the presence of Bolingbroke (a Lancastrian heir) there and the birth there of his son.

The castle underwent the usual rejuvenation, after the usual period of Tudor neglect, during the Civil War. It was taken by alternate sides and finally fell to the Parliamentarians, a blow which marked the beginning of the downfall of the Royalists of which the fall of Raglan was to provide the end. Cromwell's army made a better job of pulling it down than they did of Raglan, and when the war and the subsequent Republic were both over, and things returned to normal, the Marquis of Worcester built what is now Great Castle House out of the ruins, in 1673. This fine and well-preserved building, which contains some remarkable decorated ceilings, now houses the Royal Monmouthshire Royal Engineers (Militia).

A glimpse of the castle can be had, with some difficulty, from the back streets below, and what is left of it gives the outline impression of a sturdy and compact fortress. Monmouth in general retains, more than many ancient towns, its feeling of being old-established. Possibly this is the result of its having kept intact its medieval street pattern; or perhaps it is that the character of the town, a country, farming centre, set in the middle of riverside fields, has clearly never altered. All around stretch the long levels of river meadows, the proper season of which is high summer, buttercup and cow-parsley time, a time of midge-ridden rural summer afternoons.

The streets have the healthy look caused both by the presence of so much air and light, and by their occupation by unmistakably bright-cheeked country people. The large number of licensed premises alone would lead one to deduce an old and strongly communal settlement, a perfectly accurate conclusion about this typical market town, which, like so many of its kind, is the sort of place in which everybody knows a great deal about everybody else. The people and the town share the substantial confidence of a prosperous farming country. And who would not feel confident, being the owner of some Monmouthshire acres, on, say, a fine November day, when the meet is at the Walnut

THE WYE   201

Tree and that pale blue haze is above the river.

Unlike some rivers the Wye dominates its valley, which (below Monmouth) is all sloping banks and water. The green silky river fills its bottom. It loops and wanders, through its backdrops of oak woods, in the leisured geodesics of a true-bred river valley. The concise and tree-choked outlook is so Welsh that it is inconceivable that one side of it belongs to England. But the fact is that the river Wye is a beautiful and lazy national boundary, and Gloucestershire farm-houses and cottages look down from the sun-soaked eastern bank onto the shade and cool depths of Welsh woodlands.

Nothing more urban than a couple of tiny villages disturbs this idyll. One comes to Tintern down the valley lulled and softened by scenery, and the soaring and spectacular abbey buildings stand out as, if not actually inappropriate, at least a prominent deviation from the context. Man does not otherwise obtrude in the Wye valley – his houses are brown and low, and squat close into the folds of fields – and the way Tintern rears and soars against the wooded hills and the lush green fields makes something of an impact which, for all the professed humility and retreat of monastic life, cannot have been totally unintended. Those exalted walls and high clerestories, the sublime loftiness of it all, the reaching, everywhere, it seems, after even greater heights – nothing about it speaks of a retreat from the human, social world, or a prostration of one's identity before the world's creator. There is no genuflexion about Tintern, and what reverence there is seems rather to be of celebration than of obeisance. If it worships anything which we can recognize, standing today among the cows and thistledown, it is the extreme expansion of the human spirit, which has shown itself able, by the application of so much dedicated endeavour, to take a permanent form in stone.

How could, one wonders, a civilized Renaissance monarch ever have brought himself, even for strong political reasons, to dissolve these monasteries, knowing as he must have done what physical form this act must take – the stripping of the lead roofs, for instance, and the consequent sudden ruin of buildings such as Tintern. It is true, of course, that by 1536 the Cistercians had become largely an earthly, money-oriented body. The study and meditation of earlier centuries had become obscured and to a large extent replaced by the concerns of land-owning. But up to the Dissolution Tintern had at least remained in use since its original foundation, on a smaller scale, some four hundred years before.

The first Cistercian abbey in this quiet and fertile valley was built in 1131, a colony of Norman monks, in their identifying habits of white cloth, coming to occupy it from L'Aumone, which was an off-shoot of the monastery at Citeaux from which the order took its name. Not much beyond the ground-plan of this early church remains, and the grandiose high-vaulted building which grew up around it came into existence during the late thirteenth century. It was largely finished, however, by 1301, so that the ruins which we have there now are contemporary with the great medieval castles of which these strong, well-structured walls are so reminiscent.

After the Dissolution the site of the church was occupied by a pioneering metal business, which was powered by a stream which at this point runs into the Wye, and which at an early date produced the alloy of copper and zinc that, as brass, has subsequently played so large a part among metals. The ruins themselves attracted little attention, and grew overgrown and inaccessible, until a more romantic age found a new use for such mysterious, ivy-draped outcrops of Gothic splendour. Such as are shown, for example, in Turner's water-colour of these Abbey ruins. Wordsworth best exemplifies, perhaps, the apotheosis of the monuments in wild, overgrown countryside, which this new-found attitude bestowed on places such as Tintern.

"No poem of mine," he wrote, "was composed under circumstances more pleasant for me to remember than this. I began it upon leaving Tintern, after crossing the Wye, and concluded it just as I was entering Bristol in the evening, after a ramble of four or five days with my sister."

"Tintern Abbey" — more correctly, but rather inconveniently, called "Lines composed a few miles above Tintern Abbey, on revisiting the banks of the Wye during a Tour. July 13, 1798." — was published in *Lyrical Ballads* the same autumn. It is 159 lines long, and like so many of his poems, being very uneven, would have benefited by some discriminating editing. The following is perhaps the nearest one can get to a favourable sample.

> If this
> Be but a vain belief, yet, oh! how oft —
> In darkness and amid the many shapes
> Of joyless daylight; when the fretful stir
> Unprofitable, and the fever of the world,
> Have hung upon the beatings of my heart —
> How oft, in spirit, have I turned to thee,
> O sylvan Wye! thou wanderer thro' the woods,
> How often has my spirit turned to thee!
>
> And now, with gleams of half-extinguished thought,
> With many recognitions dim and faint,
> And somewhat of a sad perplexity,
> The picture of the mind revives again:·
> While here I stand, not only with the sense
> Of present pleasure, but with pleasing thoughts,
> That in the moment there is life and food
> For future years.

For much of the poem one wonders simply how he got away with it. Did his readers really want to know so much about his personal inner ponderings, many of which are relevant to little other than his life-long autobiographical investigation? Little of "Tintern Abbey" is directly concerned with, or even emanates from, the Wye, the Abbey ruins, or anything accessible to the people to whom he presumably addressed his remarks; and when, for the last forty lines or so, he concerns himself with expressing his emotional relationship with his sister, it is hard not to feel that there are more interesting considerations which might have been generated by these evocative ruins in the Wye valley.

To come down out of the spiritual realms of Tintern and into the outskirts of Chepstow may quite often seem like a return to reality, a waking from those Wordsworthian dreams which the Wye valley so irresistibly induces. Not that

Chepstow, with its castle and its old town walls, is particularly representative of the present. But from the racecourse
onwards one feels onself to be in a busy modern world,
traffic-ridden, commercial, untidily congested.

Chepstow itself, an active and quite cheerful town on the
slope of a steep hill, is on the Wye, which at this point runs,
largely out of sight among undistinguished houses, under the
cliffs of an escarpment. Through Chepstow the Wye comes to
its mouth in the larger waters of the Severn, and the area has,
apart from Chepstow's age-old function as a commercial
centre, a tradition of ship-repairing.

The gate of the town's medieval wall, and a few remaining
narrow streets, provide a hazy memory of its ancientness. But
to a large extent this characteristic has been subsequently
obscured by jumbled and inconsistent architecture and
planning. The massive castle lies below the town, on the river
bank, the stronghold of the Marcher Lords in whose hands
the town and district lay. The early Norman castle here was
rebuilt during the thirteenth century, and must have served
the function of protecting an important line of communication. Because of its position at the junction of rivers, the
town has always been connected with routes and bridges.

The crossing of the Wye at Chepstow, by Brunel's tubular
suspension bridge, formed a significant step in the opening up
of South Wales; it linked the Great Western Railway with the
South Wales line, much as the Heads of the Valleys road now
links the industrial area with the main British motorway
system. The lower Wye, at this point, has the additional
feature of having a bore, like the Severn, and the distinction
of possessing possibly the greatest tidal range in Britain, with
reputed 53-foot springs.

Chepstow has its racecourse on the one side, the largest in
Wales, and on the other the spread of the Severn opening into
the Bristol Channel. The coastal country is flat and rather
viewless, field-trees and hedges spreading across silted plains.
The Roman Road running to Caerwent passes under the
Motorway which sweeps towards the Severn Bridge. And
nearby, in the fields, Caldicot Castle sits among its elderly
yews.

In a restored part of this rambling and unpretentious

ancient monument take place each weeknight those strangely
fashionable anachronisms of the later twentieth century, the
raucous and gluttonous occasions known as Medieval Ban-
quets.

Coming from Chepstow down to Caldicot one catches
glimpses, from time to time, of the monumental towers
which bear the cables which suspend the Bridge. So swift has
the change been, the change in our attitudes and expectations, that the days when we used to take the creaking ferry,
(rather than opt for the 60-mile drive around the head of the
river by the nearest crossing-place at Gloucester), are scarcely
even over when they have already come to seem to us
prehistoric. Down that suicidal slithering concrete bank on
one side, with the sharp turn, uncomfortably close to the
lapping water, onto the swaying boat; across the spray-
throwing, pitching, choppy grey water of the estuary, and
eventually up the other vertical-seeming bank. The memory
of it contrasts strangely with the sight, now, of those
thousands of vehicles sweeping across the water some
hundred and twenty feet below them.

The bridge had been planned since the 1840s, and after
several proposals during the nineteenth century had failed to
achieve acceptance, more serious consideration was given to
the matter during the 1920s. The county councils concerned
had managed to form a joint committee by 1936, but things
still went slowly. A crossing-point was finally agreed in 1945,
and a design then commissioned. Still nothing actually
happened, however, and discussions continued through the
1950s. After the building of the Forth Bridge the designs for
the Severn one were radically modified, and, in order to
make the best use of experience, the same firms were
transferred, in the 1960s, to start work at Beachley and Aust.
Nobody concerned could be accused of impetuosity, since it
had by then taken a hundred and fifteen years to make the
decision to start.

The bridge itself is only a part of a whole complex, which
includes a viaduct at Beachley and a shorter bridge continuing over the Wye. Thus though the construction of the
Severn Bridge cost eight million pounds, and took a little
over five years to complete, the whole business of which it

forms a part is estimated to have cost between fifteen and sixteen million. It was started in 1961 and opened by the Queen in September 1966.

The structure's design relies principally on its cables. These carry the load of the deck and its cargo by means of anchors pulling them down, and thus transforming a tension in one direction into a pull in another. The cable is of high tensile steel wire, consisting of more than 8,000 wires compressed into a cylinder form of 20 inches diameter. The two 400-foot-high towers support them, and they are linked to the suspended deck by 340 single-stranded cables made of galvanized steel wires which are set at 60-foot intervals at an angle to the deck, forming a sequence of triangles. The deck itself, thus hanging, is a hollow steel box made up of 88 sections, and made in a shallow, aeroplane-wing shaped design, to reduce wind resistance.

The bridge, completed, is a toll-bridge, and also incorporates cycle and pedestrian sections cantilevered out from the main structure. It is 105 feet wide in all, with a main span of 3,240 feet and two side spans each of 1,000. It has already done much to relieve congestion on both banks of the estuary, and has opened up commercial and industrial possibilities in the West Country as well as in South Wales. In spite of all this it is now envisaged that a second bridge may eventually be necessary, possibly even as soon as the 1980s.

For the time being it continues to provide a spectacle as a modern wonder. If this is what the new age looks like, then it has at least got the merit of visual splendour. Much as one may regret, in principle at least, the violent urgency which now propels us, the need we feel to speed from place to place with the least possible contact with our surroundings, the pressure on us to fit into one day as many different undertakings as we can — even so the hurrying, frantic particles of this total scheme are dwarfed by the soaring monuments to which they have given rise. Formal, immobile, complete, the Severn Bridge springs out of the confusion; elegant steel sweeping in one expansive movement into England.

CONCLUSION

DIVERSITY AND UNITY

About seven and a half thousand square miles accounts for Wales from top to bottom. It is not a large place, and one would not be particularly surprised to be told that there are farms, in some more spacious countries, which are about the same size. The whole of the population of two and three-quarter million would nowadays just about suffice to occupy a major city. Yet the variation of character within this scope is as great as that of the regions of France. In the broad distinctions of north, mid, and south, to begin with, it is as if several different countries were making use of the same label, "Wales".

The differences of impression are even more striking within a smaller context, within an area one might naturally take to be a unit. South Wales is about forty miles long by a maximum of a hundred miles wide. What can you hope to find in a place that size?

A conjuring-trick pulls out of the impossibly small container the ludicrous profusion of doves and rabbits, in reply. A pattern of alternation again sets itself up, to provide, on an even smaller scale, a structure of internal tensions. The cliffs of Pembrokeshire counterpart the farm country of Carmarthen within the area, distinct in itself, which is generally known as West Wales. The mammoth works of Margam and Swansea's suburban sprawl exist as if to counterpoint the primal woodlands, hilltops, and desert-island bays of Gower. Contrapuntal again are the themes of sandstone and limestone which run through the Brecon Beacons, the one providing broad and open sweeps of treeless country, the other the cluttered and cracked groupings of gorges, knolls, falling streams and valley scrub.

One cannot even say that the Valleys are free of it, of this argument of character which makes the place so rich. The remnants of major industry and of dense population sit, as if by the result of montage, in beautiful and open hill country. The same effect is differently produced by the placing of the Cardiff-Newport complex on the margin of the Vale of Glamorgan's lovely landscapes. And even within this there are poignant points of contrast such as that of Barry and Llantwit, or Porthcawl and Merthyr Mawr.

Perhaps only the eastern part of Gwent, that appendage which for so long was so awkwardly stuck on, in the form 'and-Monmouthsire', to the Principality's rear, belies its Welshness, marks itself as border-country, by lacking an overall spirit of inner contradiction.

Because that if anything — the ambiguity and resistance to classification, the constant provision of the unexpected, the refusal to be straightforward and predictable — is what makes Wales Welsh. It is hard to find any other quality, in fact, which Bangor shares with Pontypridd, or even Brecon with Llanelli or Cowbridge with Manorbier.

If Wales's physical make-up is characterized by its complexity, so, to some extent, the people themselves are unified by their immutable refusal to drop neatly into slots. An over-simplified view of them, no matter what it is, could only be held by someone able to ignore a great part of the evidence. They are not ethnically distinct; they never were. The small dark, lively people of the stereotype were only, at any stage, a sub-group sharing the territory with other groups which were equally consistently tall and fair. The invasion by metal-working nations during the last thousand years before the birth of Christ (tribes which can meaningfully be called the Celts, because they brought the Celtic language and culture from its Continental home) was neither the first nor the last such wave of new population.

Roman colonization introduced further Continental influences. No doubt the soldiers, who themselves had probably been gathered from all parts of Europe, left some of their genes behind. Irish influence was pouring all the time into Pembrokeshire. The English (for want of a better name for that diverse agglomeration of tribes from Jutland and Schleswig-Holstein) mainly played the part of a limiting factor on the gloomier bank of Offa's dyke. The Normans however, who, as their name records, were really a Viking colony resident in northern France, infiltrated, occupied, and greatly affected much of South Wales. To add to the existing confusion they brought in Flemish colonists to inhabit Pembrokeshire. Since then industrialization has provided an enticement, and around the docks of Swansea, Cardiff and Newport immigrant labour from all the countries of the world which have large ports has settled and accumulated like silt, and has been drawn into the hinterland of industry and housing and even, during times of economic change, up into the valleys.

With all that flood of national and racial origin how, one might wonder, is it possible to talk about the Welsh. How could one say, for instance, "Wales for the Welsh", without inviting the reaction "What for the who?" Quite easily, it so happens, and without even any imprecision.

It is well known that if you analyse anything carefully enough it disappears. Often we have to face the slightly disconcerting discrepancy between the sum of a thing's parts and the thing as a whole. Water, for instance, unlike its elements, does not float off into the air, explode, or promote combustion. Wales is not a hotch-potch of people living in a jumble of places, but a single definite, and easily recognizable thing. What is more, although inevitably north and south will continue to compete and to dismiss or insult each other as they always have done, it is implicit even in this garden-fence quarrel that they are united in their joint and intransigent Welshness.

The conclusion which one comes to as a result of a close knowledge of South Wales, of its history, make-up, people and present circumstances, is that characteristics, like matter, are ultimately indestructible. It is as if one had thought, for instance, that by diluting oil with water one could get rid of it, could make it somehow no longer oil. Take an existing social and geographical unit, see what you can do. Pour in Norman Lords, English armies, Shropshire iron-masters, Staffordshire workers, immigrant settlers, international industries, foreign tourists, European policies. What are you left with?

Wales.

Just as Merthyr Tydfil, once it had arisen as a chance result of the existence of iron-ore at the edge of the coalfield, continued, while Guest converted Dowlais to making steel and while modern policy has switched the town's production over to Hoover's, to remain doggedly and unequivocally in existence; so, once a thing has formed itself, there seems to be a natural law militating for ever against its disintegration. It can become bad or good, but it cannot become non-existent.

In the case of South Wales this perpetuation of identity has taken a partly social, partly economic form. There is something that one might call a South Wales attitude, which runs through all its diversity: an attitude of good-will and openness which adds to the already considerable attractions of the country for the visitor. The economic aspect of its nature exists in the fact that it is, whatever one may like to think, the centre-of-wealth of Wales as a whole. Wales, like England, is bottom-heavy. Most of the rest of it is poor.

In this respect South Wales has another interesting point to make. That is, that industry and urban life need not have the unbeautifying effect with which they are normally associated. South Wales has not, in the long run, based its conceptions on the rigid separation which is so often applied – in which everything rural is good and nice, everything industrial by corollary being squalid and unpleasant. The reconditioned areas, for instance, make it clear that it is possible for nature and industry to live in a state of symbiosis. (You give us coal from your subterranean seams; after a lapse of a hundred years or so we give you new forests for your hillsides). But more than this, in areas where industry is not a relic but a reality, it is clear that it is possible for scenery and factories to co-exist, if not in complete marital harmony at least in a state of mutual neutrality.

In any case the problem is not by any means a large one. Only a small corner of South Wales is, or ever was, industrialized. Only a patch even of that is really urban. It will be clear to anyone who has read as far as this that the real nature of the country, spacially, is agricultural. Vast areas of it are all rich and wholesome farmland. Even more of it, perhaps, is open hill pasture full of larks, ponies, and views.

Nevertheless man is a social animal, and not on the whole given to solitude. He constructs much of his existence jointly, and one of his best achievements is the town. In this respect, too, South Wales had done pretty well. The town as a living and evolving thing has many instances there, where old settlements like Kidwelly, Carmarthen, or Monmouth, middle-aged ones such as Merthyr and Porthcawl, and brand new places like Cwmbran or Aberavon, all fulfil the same requirement, being vehicles for the socialness of the life of the country. A place, that is, where one can meet people in the street.

An enormous amount of conversation takes place in South Wales. In that, as in several of its qualities, it provides a rival to Ireland. It is part, perhaps, of the identity of the community; people know and interact with each other, and consequently jointly come to share a feeling of belonging to a certain place. This quality, a sort of correspondence of people and places, is a strong South Wales characteristic, and, almost paradoxically, is not something which they can lose even by leaving. And because life is economic as well as social there are indeed many instances of leaving.

The cultural life of the country in particular has suffered from the greater rewards offered by English culture. Geoffrey of Monmouth left. Giraldus Cambrensis left. W. H. Davies left. Dylan Thomas left. And yet they each helped to prove a point even by these departures, since they still retained a feeling of belonging to South Wales; and, given the opportunity, they came back.

What is really interesting, of course, about a place, town or country, is what it means to the people who live and work in it, or on it. There seems to be in South Wales this feeling of a need to relate to a location, to make it part of oneself. Only if they had failed to take account of this sort of need, which on the whole they have not, would the new towns and all the redevelopments of older ones have failed.

These too, these remodelled places, with their new shopping-centres and their pedestrian streets, their new factories around the edge, and, in almost every case, their old castle in the middle, show every sign of being intrinsically adaptable enough to cope with whatever future it turns out to be. That, of course, is unpredictable, just as, we can now see, the sudden changes of the past could not really have been foreseen by the people who found themselves adapting, with the discomfort and agility of contortionists, to something which had turned out to be quite different from what had been expected. So that one could not really have said, for instance, "the Normans will be coming; we must prevent them from making castles", or "when steel is invented, our iron-works will be in the wrong place", any more than one could say for certain now that making car-bodies is no occupation for the 1980s, or that oil refineries are likely to become eventually little more than monstrous tourist attractions. We do not know such things with sufficient certainty to be able to base our actions on them.

What is certain is that South Wales shows no sign, in the immediate future, of declining in importance, in interest, or in attraction. Every aspect of it gives the same impression of being well-established, and whether or not material prosperity, which is often little more than a receding mirage, can ever securely be achieved, the place will remain one which, within a small area, has a large amount to offer.

BIBLIOGRAPHY

Early History and Mythology
Ashe, G., *From Caesar to Arthur*, 1960, London, Collins
Geoffrey of Monmouth (trans. Lewis Thorpe), *The History of the Kings of Britain*, 1966, London, Penguinn
Gruffydd, W. J., *Rhiannon — an inquiry into the First and Third Branches of the Mabinogi*, 1953, Cardiff, University of Wales Press
Jones, G. and T. (eds. and trans.), *The Mabinogion*, 1957, London, Dent (Everyman)
Rees, A. and B., *Celtic Heritage*, 1961, London, Thames & Hudson
Rees, W., *A Historical Atlas of Wales*, 1959, London, Faber & Faber

Ancient Monuments
Official Guidebooks, London, H.M.S.O.:
    Carreg Cennen Castle, 1972
    Kidwelly Castle, 1972
    Raglan Castle, 1970
    Tintern Abbey, 1964
A Short History of Pembroke Castle, 1971, Tenby, The Five Arches Press
The Roman Legionary Fortress at Caerleon, 1963, Cardiff, National Museum of Wales

Industrialization
Dodd, A. H., *Life in Wales*, 1972, London, Batsford
Humphrys, G., *Industrial Britain: South Wales*, 1972, London, David and Charles
Minchinton, W. E. (ed.), *Industrial South Wales 1750-1914: Essays in Welsh Economic History*, 1969, London, Cass

National Parks

Pembrokeshire and the National Park, Tenby, H. G. Walters Ltd

Davies, M. (ed.), *Brecon Beacons National Park*, 1972, London, H.M.S.O.

Places of Interest

Official Guides:

The Dan-yr-Ogof Caves, Swansea, W. Walters & Son Ltd

St Fagans, 1973, Cardiff, National Museum of Wales

Hoare, I., *The Severn Bridge Souvenir Handbook*, Cheltenham, Maudersley Press Ltd

Mansel Thomas, J. (ed.), *A Guide to Gower*, 1965, Swansea, Crown Printers

Literature

Brinnin, J. M., *Dylan Thomas in America*, 1960, London, Harborough (Ace Books)

Davies, W. H., *The Autobiography of a Super-Tramp*, 1924, London, Cape

Giraldus Cambrensis, *The Itinerary Through Wales, Description of Wales*, 1935, London, Dent (Everyman)

John, A. *Chiaroscuro. Fragments of Autobiography*, 1952, London, Cape

Tedlock, E. W. (ed.), *Dylan Thomas, The Legend and the Poet*, 1960, London, Heinemann

Thomas, D., *Under Milk Wood*, 1957, London, Dent

Collected Poems, 1956, London, Dent

A Prospect of the Sea, 1955, London, Dent

Quite Early One Morning, 1954, London, Dent

INDEX